THE EMERGING CONSENSUS . . . ?

INSTITUTE OF ECONOMIC AFFAIRS

The Institute was formed in 1957 as a research and educational trust that specialises in the study of markets and pricing systems as technical devices for registering preferences and apportioning resources. Micro-economic analysis forms the kernel of economics and is relevant and illuminating in both government and private sectors, in collectivist as well as in individualist societies. Where the macro-economic method is used its results are verified and interpreted in the light of micro-economic significance.

The Institute's work is assisted by an advisory council:

The Institute is independent of any political party or group and financed by sales of publications and by voluntary contributions from individuals, organisations and companies.

Details of IEA publications are available from:

2 Lord North Street, Westminster, London SW1P 3LB
Telephone: 01-799 3745

THE EMERGING CONSENSUS . . . ?

Essays on the interplay between ideas, interests and circumstances in the first 25 years of the IEA

Ralph Harris Arthur Seldon

GRAHAM HUTTON T. W. HUTCHISON

D. P. O'BRIEN JAMES M. BUCHANAN

GORDON TULLOCK A. J. CULYER DAVID COLLARD

KEN JUDGE IAN BRADLEY COLIN CLARK

LORD CROHAM ERIC SHARP NORMAN GASH

John B. Wood

Edited by ARTHUR SELDON

Published by
THE INSTITUTE OF ECONOMIC AFFAIRS
1981

First published in June 1981 by
THE INSTITUTE OF ECONOMIC AFFAIRS
2 Lord North Street, London SW1P 3LB

ISBN 0-255 36141-6 (cased edition)
ISBN 0-255 36142-4 (paperback edition)

Printed in England by
Goron Pro-Print Co. Ltd., Lancing, West Sussex
Text set in Monotype Times Roman 11 on 12pt.

CONTENTS

FOREWORD

The Emerging Consensus . . . ?

by Lord Harris of High Cross

The Founding Fathers of the IEA shared no narrow orthodoxy. Rather the reverse: they saw themselves as resisting the advance of a cramping consensus that would end in a corporatist conformity of ruling élites and interest-groups.

By 1957 there was already a tendency to scorn the 'old economics of scarcity'. Even professional economists would judge alternative proposals less on their merits for improving the use of scarce resources than by their convenience to politicians in 'running the economy'. It was easily assumed that if only well-intentioned politicians were armed with more power they would infallibly advance the 'public interest'.

Twenty-five years later it is easier to see why Mr Samuel Brittan has mocked 'Government' as a 'magic organisation' expected to solve every problem. Indeed, the failure of Labour and Conservative administrations to achieve their most cherished aims has begun to sow doubts about the unmixed benevolence of unlimited government. Yet the free society depends ultimately on strong governmental authority, not least to protect the community against the perennial challenge of sectional producer interests.

To restore this necessary authority to government requires a more enduring consensus about its essential responsibilities, as distinct from those of individuals and families in a free society. To avoid disappointment or disillusion, we need better understanding of the long-term cost of trying to placate sectional interest-groups by pursuing popular policies that are mutually inconsistent, or even self-destructive. And we have ceaselessly to explore ways of freeing politicians for their essential duties, by relieving them of tasks that could be better performed by voluntary co-operation to serve the general consumer interest through competitive markets.

It is as a further contribution to clarifying such issues that we offer this discussion of the IEA's work during the last quarter of a century.

April 1981 RALPH HARRIS

Preamble

THE ESSENCE OF THE IEA

Arthur Seldon

This collection of essays, most by economists, historians of economic thought, economic and political historians and a sociologist of a wide range of philosophic sympathies, assesses the IEA and its work over 25 years against a background of changing economic thinking and public policy. An introduction to the essays may also serve as a short re-statement of the IEA's central approach, from which some IEA authors will differ.

The essays range over British history to consider the interactions between the influence of ideas, emphasised by J. M. Keynes as ruling the world, vested interests, singled out by Karl Marx as the dominant element, and 'circumstances', identified by J. S. Mill as deciding which ideas would influence events. The classic illustration is Lenin who spent a lifetime of proselytizing before the First World War provided the 'circumstances' for his ideas. (*Pace* Marx, 'interests' were secondary or remote.) Four mainly historical chapters, by Professor T. W. Hutchison, Dr Ian Bradley, Dr Colin Clark and Professor Norman Gash, re-examine the past century for parallels with earlier efforts to educate by research and dissemination the general public and the men of ideas and of action who evolved and applied economic thinking. Professor Hutchison further discusses the IEA's dual emphasis on a general economic diagnosis with detailed proposals suited to the institutional conditions of the times.

Five essays analyse more closely and appraise the products of the IEA, with reservation as well as approval from Professors Denis O'Brien, Anthony Culyer and David Collard and Mr Kenneth Judge, and with suggestions for further development from Professors J. M. Buchanan and Gordon Tullock. Two chapters judge the IEA's work as seen by Lord Croham from inside government and by Mr Eric Sharp from inside industry. Mr Graham Hutton, an early stalwart, discusses the pre- and post-war thinking on economics that dissatisfied the Founding Fathers of the IEA and induced them to examine its errors and consequences in industrial and public policy.

These essays are for readers to judge in the light of the IEA's work over 25 years. Any credit must go largely to the 300 economists, political scientists and other authors and to the advisers who were ready with suggested names of possible authors and subjects. Although the IEA staff have contributed to this published output, most of the Papers, etc., are the work of British economists in British universities. The IEA drew on a wide range of academic authority (and philosophic sympathy) without which it could not have maintained the flow of writing that has made it the largest source of concentrated but digestible economic expertise in Britain.

The IEA may perhaps claim to have created the post-war focus for the demonstration that market analysis was indispensable for understanding and solving economic tasks and problems. Its authors included economists sophisticated in mathematical macro-economic models of the economy as a whole (not least Colin Clark, who privately pioneered national income statistics), but IEA Papers showed that macro-economic analysis of national (or average) behaviour had to be explained by micro-economic analysis of individuals moved by changes at the margin of effort or reward. In particular, because we at the IEA were unconvinced from the outset by the Fabians, Keynes, Beveridge and Titmuss, we systematically mustered and presented in modern dress the truths of classical political economy: that government could not assemble the information required for the desired use of resources; that only individuals could derive the information from their local, voluntary, private lives; that they could reveal and apply the information only or most effectively by coming together as buyers and sellers in markets.

THE NEW IEA APPROACH

This indeed was and is the essence of the IEA approach, and why it struck early observers as a fundamental break from the dominant but misguided post-war consensus (below). Although the approach has a noble intellectual lineage in the English and Scottish classical economists and philosophers from David Hume and Adam Smith, it had been overshadowed if not obliterated by the emphasis on national ('macro-economic') policy from the Great Depression of 1929-31 to the apparent effectiveness of Keynesian demand management in mastering unemployment before the Second World War and inflation after the war. From these apparent successes the belief developed that government could deal with any and every economic problem by regulation or direct management: not only in defence, law and order, and the supply of money but also in fuel and transport, education and medicine, housing and pensions, local services and everywhere else.

The IEA approach was very different. It began from the very opposite end of the economic pyramid: the large number of individuals organised in families, voluntary groups, co-operative organisations, one-man businesses, partnerships or firms. It recognised that some goods or services—the so-called 'public goods'—had to be supplied by government, national or local, and financed by taxes or rates, because they could not be refused to people who refused to pay and who would otherwise batten on those who did pay by taking 'free rides'. But for the rest it opened up questions that had lain dormant for decades. Why should this or that service be supplied by government? Why could it not be supplied by people coming together in 'markets' where those who wanted things could choose between those who offered them? If markets were not feasible, was that because choice for buyers or competition among suppliers was impracticable, or because government itself was putting legal or other obstacles in the way of individuals with goods or services to exchange?

If markets were impracticable, what other method of co-operation between buyers and suppliers was feasible? Was it better to construct state monopolies—as in fuel or transport, education or medicine—and try to arrange that they served buyers faithfully and efficiently?

Or did such organisations have their own weaknesses of political and impersonal control, bureaucratic inflexibility, high taxation and restriction of choice between suppliers? If markets were practicable, how could the obstacles to them be removed?

In opening up these prospects the IEA released a shoal of questions that to many early observers seemed closed and settled. The very first Paper in 1957 asked not how the state could best finance its 'national insurance' pensions but why pensions had to be supplied by, or rather through, the state at all: why should they not gradually move from the state to the market, where suppliers were developing a wide variety of schemes to suit individuals and firms with much more flexibility than the state could arrange? That the state may have considered it desirable, on the grounds of poverty in 1908 or the high cost of approved societies in 1925, to develop state pensions was no reason for continuing and enlarging them in 1957. Yet the Labour Party was proposing to extend state pensions in 1957 and the Conservatives extended them in 1961.

SOME FUNDAMENTAL ECONOMIC TRUTHS

And so on in scores and hundreds of Papers on many more services and activities. A barrage of IEA Papers refined and applied old truths to new subjects in contemporary circumstances. Authors were asked to apply economic analysis ruthlessly, with recognition of current conditions but without regard for 'administrative practicability', because that could not be ascertained except by practical trial, or for 'political impossibility', because that could be a pretext developed by politicians or bureaucrats who resisted reform that did not suit them however good the argument, and in any event because reasoned ideas could themselves make the 'impossible' possible.

In pursuing these new/old approaches to new subjects IEA Papers illustrated from contemporary events and developments the fundamental truths of economics that had been often lost in the preoccupation with post-war monetary or fiscal measures to control inflation or unemployment. Production takes place for consumption (derived from the Scot Adam Smith), not the other way round. Value is measured not as an average but at the margin (the Englishman W. S. Jevons, the Frenchman Leon Walras, and the Austrian Carl Menger). The cost of producing a commodity or service is not the labour required (the German Karl Marx) but the commodity or service thereby lost (the Austrian Friedrich von Wieser). The instinct of man is to 'truck and barter' in markets (Adam Smith). He will find ways round, under, over or through restrictions created by government (the Austrian Eugen von Böhm-Bawerk). There is no such thing as absolute demand (for education, medicine or anything else) or supply (of labour or anything else) because both vary with price (the Englishmen Alfred Marshall, Lionel Robbins and many before and since). Not least, without the signalling device of price, man cannot spontaneously and voluntarily co-operate for prosperous co-existence (the Austrian Ludwig von Mises and the Austrian-born but voluntarily-British Friedrich Hayek).

Otherwise sophisticated laymen in government and industry often find difficulty with fundamental economic truths. Demand and supply are not absolute, fixed in amount; they can be elastic in response to changes in price and income—an increased demand for private education will eventually expand supply. Unemployment is not an immutable technical total; the lower the cost of labour the higher the demand for it would rise: and unemployment will fall. Cuts in government expenditure will impair government services; that is not a reason for not cutting: the economist asks whether the money would do more good elsewhere—its opportunity cost and marginal utility. Competition is the environment—the *only* environment—in which commodities or services can be judged by *comparison* with alternatives; if there is only one, how can it be judged? And competition is the *only* effective method of defending the consumer by making every seller his ally against every other seller.

THE INDISPENSABLE ROLE OF PRICE

The post-war ills of the British economy derive ultimately from the neglect of these and allied truths. Government is grossly inflated. Inefficient state monopolies hamper competitive private industry. Unnecessary growth in taxation discourages risk-taking and investment. Rampant trade unions resist the monetary mastery of inflation, the modernisation of industry, and the movement of men. Activities in which people spend other people's money and are unaccountable to them have multiplied. Unemployment is concealed by workers in the wrong jobs, in the wrong firms, in the wrong industries, in the wrong regions, because *relative* wages do not move to attract them to the right jobs, in the right firms, in the growing industries, in new regions.

The divorce of supply or demand from price in electricity, gas, rail, road, education, medicine, housing, a host of local government services, not least in labour by incomes policies, has produced massive, de-stabilising, simultaneous wastes of surpluses and shortages. The suppression or distortion of price in the public sector has annihilated the information on relative values and scarcities of resources in alternative employments without which rational or efficient use is unlikely or impossible. Government policy has fastened on the income effects and ignored the price (rationing) effects of its policies in taxation, nationalised industries, the public corporations, welfare and local government. For decades the British economy has been unhinged from the sources of grass-roots information. The repression of price is the genesis of the economic weakness, by concealing reality. Such is the case for restoring markets, where possible, in public as well as in private economic life. It is the argument for charging in public services where possible and taxing only where necessary.

Not least, the welfare state has developed, as IEA authors said in the early 1960s, into an uncontrollable monster with an insatiable appetite for tax finance and incestuous administrators. It denies choice. It substitutes incorrigible differences in cultural power which determine access in the state for corrigible differences in purchasing power which determine access in the market. It demands increasing coercion as incomes rise, as in the suppression of private education and medicine. And it is largely unaccountable and therefore irresponsible because it is run by men spending other men's money. Economists and sociologists who emphasise the external benefits of state welfare strangely overlook its external costs in tax disincentives, resistances to reform, diminished personal liberties, weakened family cohesion, and social conflict where political consensuses are enforced on minorities, groups or individuals.

THE CHALLENGE TO THE ECONOMIC ESTABLISHMENT

Many economists helped to build the IEA's reputation. Among others, Professor B. S. Yamey's (first) *Hobart Paper* on resale price maintenance in 1960 is generally thought to have prompted the debate that led to the Resale Prices Act of 1964. Colin Clark in 1961 showed the superficiality of 'growthmanship'. The *Choice in Welfare* surveys from 1963 went over the heads of politicians who said reform was 'politically impossible' and revealed high and growing demand for choice in education and medical care. The late Professor F. G. Pennance's original study of making housing subsidies 'mobile' followed in 1968. John Brunner destroyed the theoretical foundations of the 1965 National Plan. Research Monographs in 1967 rebutted the consensus on 'universal' social benefits. Professor H. S. Ferns's 1968 Paper elaborated the unassailable argument for an independent university. In 1972 nine economists and historians rejected the Marxist link between capitalism and poverty. Two Papers by John Wood in 1972 and 1975 introduced price into the discussion of unemployment and revealed the micro-unrealities in the official macro-totals. Not least, market analysis was applied to unlikely products like blood, water, fire-risks, refuse removal, animal semen, employment exchanges, charity (10 authors), sport, and the family. And several studies examined methods of supplementing low incomes, the most recent by Colin Clark in 1977.

To list these few is to be conscious of omitting

hundreds of other IEA authors (they are at least listed on pp. 271-76). The IEA was first in Britain to publicise studies in the economics of politics, government and democracy or 'public choice' (the American originators Professors Buchanan and Tullock, the British A. T. Peacock, Charles Rowley and Jack Wiseman) and of bureaucracy (Professor W. A. Niskanen). Two Papers challenged the plausible but vulnerable claim—now repeated in protests at cuts in government expenditure—that 'external benefits' justify untold expenditure on unimpeachable causes but unidentifiable benefits, from opera and the universities to space research, by the simple device of ignoring the opportunity costs. And so on, and so on, and so on.

The IEA was a substantial going concern when it published the first of several Papers by Professor Hayek in 1968 and by Professor Milton Friedman in 1970 (a Wincott Lecture attended by Mr James Callaghan) to emphasise the neglected monetary and 'Austrian' analyses of inflation and unemployment.

CONSENSUS BY COMMON INTEREST, NOT COMPROMISE WITH MYOPIA

The perennial straining after 'consensus' reflects the desire to base society on a sense of community without which it might otherwise disintegrate.

Men are consumers and producers. Their interest as consumers are general and long-term, as producers particular and immediate. The danger is that the immediate will prevail over the fundamental: that man looks through the wrong end of a telescope.

The market is the means of reconciling conflict and establishing a consensus from which all benefit. Adam

Smith's propensity to 'truck and barter' can be frustrated if government yields to pressure from organised groups of producers for protection against competition. If this short-sightedness were indulged, the economic system would end as a structure of warring groups organised as syndicates or corporations of producers protecting themselves from change. Sooner or later it would slow down and seize up. The only way to prevent this degeneration is to make the market the dominant form of organisation, so that men's interests as consumers prevail over their interests as producers. It is thus the common interest of all men to maintain the market. It is the consensus in which the long-term interest in maintaining open doors for innovation and change is shared by all as the only way to escape from stagnation and ensure progress. All other consensuses in Britain such as social contracts have required compromise with producer interests or government job creation or preservation that slowed down the adoption of improvement, retained resources in decaying industries, and prevented the rise in living standards that could have taken place, and that has taken place in the USA, Germany and Japan where men as producers have yielded to their interests as consumers in competitive markets.

The alternative is a medieval war of all against all among industrial barons, with the full panoply of restrictive practices, closed shops, demarcation, job protection, licences, permissions, permits, long patents, tariffs, quotas, and physical war, civil and international. In contrast with this world of divisiveness, the market offers co-operation by specialisation and exchange, a framework for industrial and international peacekeeping, with multi-lateral disarmament to mutual advantage. The political consensus sacrifices the long view to the short; it compromises with vested interests; it rests on the Irishism that lauds neutrality between right and wrong, good and evil. The market embodies the consensus that rests on common interests in a framework of society within which each man can do his own thing in using his talents to produce goods and services that will freely exchange for the products of his fellows.

EXPERIENCE CONFIRMED THE MARKET APPROACH

Experience of state economy is creating the readiness to learn what markets can achieve. The IEA was formed to address thinkers and doers in economic life, but since government virtually controls one-half of the economy and regulates the other half, economists must address politicians and their officials. It is evidently necessary for a people to suffer the consequences of suppressing markets before they are ready to see it as the most natural and civilised form of human co-operation. What the late Professor T. S. Ashton said in 1948 of the absence of industrialisation is still true today in the 1980s of countries which try to live without the markets that facilitate and follow industrial innovation:

> 'There are today on the plains of India and China men and women, plague-ridden and hungry, living lives little better, to outward appearance, than those of the cattle that toil with them by day and share their places of sleep by night. Such Asiatic standards, and such unmechanised horrors, are the lot of those who increase their numbers without passing through an industrial revolution.'[1]

[1] *The Industrial Revolution, 1760-1830,* Home University Library, OUP, 1948.

But since 1948 the people of China who left for Taiwan and who today escape to Hong Kong know that markets have saved them, but not their countrymen, from their former horrors. The people of India have yet to be saved. And the communist governments of Poland and Eastern Europe know that the market could save their peoples from famine and impoverishment but dare not tolerate it widely for fear it would destroy their precarious political power. In Britain, after long suppression, markets are coming to be understood in all schools of thought as information-gatherers and distributors that enthrone the consumer, reward the responsible and responsive producers, and teach the outmoded to change course. It will emerge as the dominant instrument of economic policy when it divides people in all parties who understand it from those who cannot. Market-oriented governments will then alternate in Britain as state economy recedes in Russia, China and the rest of the world and the market oases spread to fertilise the desert of state economy.

STORE OF IDEAS TO BE TESTED

So far not much has been done to re-introduce markets into the mass of British economic activity unnecessarily controlled by government or to encourage their stronger growth elsewhere by removing the obstacles to the technological innovation and *embourgeoisement* that would undermine monopoly in industry or trade unionism. There is thus a large store of ideas in IEA writings that no British government has yet applied—or tested by experiment. IEA Papers have argued that government could withdraw from many activities (perhaps two-thirds) that are not 'public goods' and leave them to local, voluntary and private competitive activity in the market. There are large, hopeful, liberating, popular reforms in the British economy that could be made by a government of any party or coalition that explained how its policies could reach the objectives.

We can say this with some justification because the field researches sponsored by the IEA (and carried out by an independent organisation) uncovered trends in the real state of public preferences that throw doubt on much accepted prejudice. The characteristic case is public attitudes to the National Health Service. Conventional opinion polling since the war has repeatedly returned favourable opinions of 80 to 90 per cent. Such statistics have misled public men for 20 years or more. First-year economics students know it is meaningless to measure demand without reference to price. The IEA field studies introduced the price of the NHS and alternative health services. The results were very different. In all socio-occupational groups they found increasing *dis*-approval of the NHS personal services—as a whole from 30 per cent in 1965 to 57 per cent in 1978 as measured by the readiness to pay for a choice of insurable private medicine by adding out of pocket to refunded taxation in the form of a voucher worth two-thirds of the insurance cost. For education the percentage rose from 30 to 51 per cent for a voucher worth two-thirds of day secondary school fees. (The results are analysed in detail in *Over-Ruled on Welfare*, 1979.)

Other findings indicated an increasing rejection of the state or its local agents in a widening range of the services it supplies as a bureaucratic monopoly in return for taxes: housing, pensions, and local welfare, and around 80 per cent in favour of allowing people who wished to contract out of state education and medicine.

These findings await a government that will heed the implications: that taxes can be substantially reduced, personal and family liberties strengthened, and the efficiency of welfare and other services improved by introducing consumer choice between competing suppliers.

THE OUTSIDE FROM THE INSIDE

The 12 Chapters have been written by 'outsiders' concerned principally with ideas and their influence on thinking and policy. Since some also discuss the IEA as an institution, an 'inside' interpretation of its beginnings is added, written by John Wood who draws on his recollections to reconstruct the early days vividly despite fragmentary documents and fading memories. Until a full history is written, his sketch, necessarily more personal than the body of the book, provides insights into the early financial and marketing tasks and how they were solved, not always fully to this day, in building the new organisation. A list of principal dates and events is added in the 'Chronology' (p. 265).

As seen from the production (editorial, etc.) side, there were parallel problems. It was rare chance that the early difficulty of discovering authors to work for an unknown, unfashionable institution made it necessary for Ralph Harris and me to work in intellectual and literary co-operation between two contrasting yet complementary minds, developing after some years into broad specialisation on production of Papers and development by fund-raising and dissemination. Commuting between two offices and dashes to clubs and restaurants by taxi to save time in the early years made the co-operation to build the embryonic fabric a breathless if exhilarating venture until a settled office and staff made possible a more systematic strategy.

The early hostility from critics and the indulgent scepticism about our prospects (the late Sir Andrew Shonfield in 1961 gave the infant IEA 'six months') must have made us marvel that we had abandoned safe jobs for a speculative venture (against which I was warned by a friendly Sir John Benn about risking a young family), though it was a mission as well as a job. The gradual building of finances while maintaining independence in order to give authors power to say what they wished was a task in chicken-and-egg timing. The earliest sense of impact, when we drew blood from the late R. H. S. Crossman in 1963 (who wrote an apology in *The Guardian* after being misled by Professor Peter Townsend), left the feeling that David could still fell Goliath. And the reaction from Mrs Shirley Williams on TV that the early welfare findings were 'nonsense' indicated that the evidence had discomforted the political consensus.

The chicken-and-egg timing is crucial. The IEA raises fundamental issues and examines new, sometimes radical, policies, and it may have to be run by two people in harness (and in harmony on ultimate goals) sufficiently strong-minded for one to raise funds but properly attribute responsibility for their disbursement on publications to the other, concerned primarily for the independence of authors. The IEA's independence from outside pressure has also throughout been reinforced by resting on general rather than earmarked funds.

Increasing interest from principled politicians in all three Parties (not one, as Mr Hugh Stephenson of

The Times[2] and others suppose) removed the anxiety that we would tend to veer to one political side to gain influential hearing. The IEA thus avoided the error of the Fabian Society (analysed by Dr Colin Clark in Chapter IX).

As the 1960s moved on, approaches were made by people in all walks of life, including Labour politicians and trade union leaders anxious about trends in public policy, one of whom said 'it's the market or machine-gun'. MPs from all three Parties addressed IEA seminars and putative leaders from all four Parties came to talk with IEA economists. Visits from former Conservative and Labour Prime Ministers encouraged the hope of competitive bidding for public support for policies based on economic reason. The fourth Party symbolises the movement in British public life away from state economy to the market.

The change from author reluctance to an increasing flow of unsolicited manuscripts (rarely used because the theme for almost all IEA Papers originates in the office) confirmed the growing sense of authority. And success in recruiting teachers, schools, libraries, universities as regular subscribers indicated the pedagogic-academic quality of IEA texts.

SOCIOLOGY BACK TO SANITY

The IEA's latest inspiration is the formation in late 1980 of a Social Affairs Unit to re-examine conventional sociological thinking on industry, welfare, and the rôles of the state and the market. Its Director, Dr Digby Anderson, lately from the University of Nottingham,

[2] *Mrs Thatcher's First Year,* Norman, 1980.

was introduced to us by Professor Dennis Lees, an early IEA author and a constant friend, and the Assistant Director, David Marsland of Brunel University, shares the view that sociology has gone sadly astray. Since the faculties of sociology in British universities have produced men who have confused rational thinking, we look to these two relatively youthful pioneers, who remind us of the spirit of the early IEA days, to undo the damage and perhaps to help sociology to become part of the intellectual enlightenment.

IDEAS REIGN OVER INTERESTS

After 25 years—for me the IEA began in 1956—my conclusion is that the combination of John Stuart Mill and J. M. Keynes was more profound than Karl Marx. The IEA sponsored, 'produced', refined and timed the ideas; insofar as they have influenced thinking (the verdict is evidently yes) or policy (so far not much), Keynes is vindicated. But 'vested interests' played no part at all in our production; nor would it have done them much good if they had: for a century market-oriented economists have been dismissed as the lackeys of the capitalists. Karl Marx stood truth on its head. Our authors drew their researches from a wide range of industrial and other sources which exerted no influence on the final published outcome because they were numerous, individually small, diverse and self-cancelling. So in the work of the IEA ideas prevailed over interests.

But if ideas were necessary, they have not proved sufficient. Mill's 'conspiring circumstances' have to bring them to life with timely intellectual and public hearing. And down the years during the 1960s and

1970s, experience of other policies taught that reform was overdue in resale price maintenance, welfare and poverty, planning, trade unions, taxation, inflation and unemployment, discussed in the stream of IEA Papers. IEA ideas increasingly synchronised with the developing disillusionment with the false wartime and post-war macro-economic consensus; they opened men's minds to new thinking, unconventional diagnoses and unfamiliar policies.

Yet if the battle of ideas is being won in the mind, the obstacles to reform remain formidable. The suppression of markets for decades has created obstruction from the interests generated by decades of error which subsist on ideas without which they are vulnerable. The hope is that the interests will see that in resisting change and reform they are mistaking short-term gains for lasting advantage: not even bureaucrats or nationalised industry chairmen or trade unions can forever resist change in the conditions of supply and demand. But the obstructing institutions may require new techniques to dismantle, with the minimum of dislocation but not too slowly since the longer the process is delayed the more disruptive it will have to be. It is in demonstrating the techniques of removing the obstacles that the IEA's next phase may chiefly lie—whether in removing the legal props or impediments, or in constitutional rules that deprive government of the temptation to yield to the obstructors, or in buying out the obstructors' accumulated expectations of income legitimised by myopic government but destructive of economic order resting on public approval.

The ultimate safeguard remains in the realm of reason. Men of action who cannot enforce their will by coercion want to believe that the argument is on their side, like the Minister for Fuel who asked: 'Do you really think we have a good case?'.[3] The truth, as so often, was seen in the 18th century by David Hume:

> 'Though man be much governed by interests, yet even interest itself, and all human affairs, are entirely governed by opinion.'

Above all the IEA was not deterred by the tired defences of established practices—'politically impossible', 'administratively impracticable', 'socially unacceptable'. Its Founding Fathers saw behind the circular reasoning, for it is ideas that can make possible, practicable and acceptable what reason shows to be desirable, timely, overdue.

STATE OR MARKET

And what is it that a century of critics have said is impossible, impracticable or unacceptable? We now see around the world the fruits of their intention—the use of political power to expand wealth-creation, regulate industry, administer social justice, abolish hardship. There are now enough comparisons and contrasts in all countries to contest the formerly unchecked claims for the state. Little wonder that where people are free to choose—in Britain, America, Australia, France, Germany, the smaller countries of Europe, Asia and Africa—they do not choose the state.

It is now less difficult to see why, when all is said, the market, where it works by opening doors to new supplies and new demands, humbles the mighty, destroys privilege, enables David to fell Goliath, equalises

[3] The policy discussed was the denationalisation of gas.

rewards, enfranchises the inarticulate, emancipates the proletarian. Because money is the irresistible leveller, the market is more democratic, more disrespectful of persons, more moral and more just than the state, which bows to and thus incites influence, faction and conspiracy to control it. By aggrandising man as consumer, the market saves society from degenerating into impoverishment by parochial syndicalism or aggressive corporatism. That is why, despite its tendency to thicken into monopoly, to generate high incomes as temporary signals of scarcities, and its slow solutions to alienation and externalities, which preoccupy some technical economists, the market remains the best hope of mankind.

March 1981 ARTHUR SELDON

Chapter I

'WHY DID IT HAPPEN . . . JUST THEN?'

Graham Hutton

The Author

GRAHAM HUTTON, born in 1904, was educated at London, French and German universities. After a First in Economics, he was called to the Bar, taught at the London School of Economics, and in 1933 joined *The Economist*. During the war he served in the Foreign Office and the Ministry of Information.

In 1948 he started business as an independent economic consultant, but combined writing, broadcasting, and serving on the boards of several companies. The best-known among his many books is a study of productivity, *We Too Can Prosper* (1953). He gave the annual Wincott Memorial Lecture in 1979, *Whatever Happened to Productivity?* (published as IEA Occasional Paper 56, 1980).

'Why Did it Happen . . . Just Then?'

In the not-so-long history of social and political thought certain turning points irregularly occur. Vulgar opinion, casting a superficial glance over humanity's social development, confuses such periodic swings of thought with 'dialectic'—though Collingwood[1] emphasised that correct 'dialectic' aims at agreement between opposites (pendulum in the middle), rather than at the mere process of swinging from one extreme to the other. If we look for some *process* in history, we run the risk—none ran it more obviously than Hegel and Marx and, later, Spengler and Toynbee—of clamping down on history (by hindsight) a fallacious framework made by a later observer, 'the observational fallacy' of natural scientists. Yet that should not preclude attempts to identify turning-points in social and political thought; to set them in their due times, places, and processes (if any); and to trace their consequences.

It is easier to do this with the biggest turning-points: the Black Death and the subsequent 'death of feudalism'; the Reformation; the coming of the absolute, secular, sovereign State; the Industrial Revolution; the Romantic era from Hegel through Marx to socialism, communism and other modern, totalitarian, social systems. Those turning-points are 'macro-events'. They work out slowly. It is harder to analyse, evaluate and

[1] *The New Leviathan*, Oxford University Press, 1942.

trace the causes and consequences of the more numerous 'micro-events': Britain's Civil War; the American and French Revolutions; the Reform Act of 1832. These worked themselves out fairly quickly, and were absorbed fairly easily into a continuum of long-run social development which permitted the longer-term 'macro-' movements to sweep on around them. Some are still sweeping on.

These thoughts serve as backcloth to the title of this Chapter. I shall try to confine it to the movements and turning points in social and political thought—here and abroad—which in the 1950-60 decade brought about in Britain the inspiration and founding of the IEA as a nucleus of new social thought, dialectic, discussion and and exposition. Other chapters by other hands are concerned with developments and changes in strictly economic thought. My concern is with the macro-currents of Western social and political thought through the last 150 years and with their micro-changes or periodic micro-consequences in Britain. Out of these last was the IEA conceived, formed and born.

TREPANNING BRITISH SKULLS

The Rev. Sydney Smith said that to get any new idea into any head of the (Bedford) Russells you would need to *trepan* it. For long—far too long, many of us would agree—you could say the same of the British as a people. If ever there *was* a 'dialectic' movement (in the vulgar sense) in the history of British social and political thought over the past two centuries, it was erratic and not regular, within narrow and not extreme limits, slow and not swift, and took an inordinately long time to work out. Adam Smith's great work, *The Wealth of*

Nations, remained un-acted-upon for two generations, and even then only minimally. The vulgar notion that *laissez-faire* in the Victorian era allowed industrialists and other businessmen to exploit 'the workers' in Britain, uncontrolled by governments and new legislation, is wildly wide of the mark. The real problem with the British as a people is not how to get good ideas *into* their skulls; it is—perhaps harder, and worse—how to get false, bad and self-destructive ideas *out*. Which brings me to ideologies.

Our century is one of ideologies. These are unproven, mainly unprovable, but unquestioningly and widely 'accepted' systems (organised patterns) of pseudo-thought, un-thought-out by their holders and acceptors. Such systems are like religious or mystical beliefs; they are systematised by their exponents and propounders, clad in emotive myths, replete with recognised rituals and comforting slogans, and operated in the social and political sphere through representatives and devotees remarkably like those in religious hierarchies. These features characterise Marxist-Leninist-Trotskyist ideology, as they do fascist, nazi or socialist ideologies—even perhaps (among economists) Keynesians and anti-Keynesians.[2] Nearly all ideologies are constructed or come into being for the attainment of *ends*—ideal States, Utopias, Heaven on earth, perfect justice, 'the good life', equality, peace, salvation. Seldom are they *aimed* at, or fashioned for, *means*. But all Hell breaks loose whenever *means* become confused with or transformed into *ends* (look at the ideologies of economists, Welfare State bureaucrats, trade unions, political parties, professional bodies).

[2] See Chapter II . . .

The social and political thought of the West *and* the East—Communist or not, democratic or not—has crystallised into a few such ideologies this century, after going through formative decades last century; and the best, fullest, deepest studies of this crystallising process have been by continental Europeans and Americans. The *locus classicus* of ideology in England is Karl Mannheim's *Ideology and Utopia*.[3] This book first appeared (in German) in 1929 and incorporated much of his seminal essays on 'Conservative Thought' (*das konservative Denken*)—the first socio-epistemological study of systematic patterns of thinking, believing and practising in German politics after the First World War—and on 'the problem of the generations' (1927) in German politics and social thought. (Incidentally, Mannheim was a Utopian Marxist at that time!)

But there were others who perceived the growing preponderance of anti-libertarian, pro-State, crypto-totalitarian ideologies in our century as it unfolded: Robert Michels's *Political Parties: a Sociological Study of the Oligarchical Tendencies of Modern Democracy* (1915);[4] Julien Benda in his *La Trahison des Clercs*[5] in the disillusionment following the First World War in the 1920s; Ortega y Gasset in his *Revolt of the Masses* at the same time; Santayana, Madariaga, and Collingwood[6] and—long before all of these, last century—James Fitzjames Stephen in his far-sighted *Liberty,*

[3] Kegan Paul (International Library of Psychology, Philosophy and Scientific Method), London, 1936. The bibliography appended is formidable and invaluable.

[4] Reprinted by the Free Press, Glencoe, Illinois, 1949.

[5] Best rendered as *Treachery of the Intellectuals.*

[6] Above, p. 3.

Equality and Fraternity remorselessly drawing out and criticising every logical implication of John Stuart Mill's *Liberty* and of Mill's socialism.

In and after the Second World War we had Hayek's famous admonitory *The Road to Serfdom* (1944), Karl Popper's *The Open Society and its Enemies* (1945) and (last but by no means least) the late-lamented J. L. Talmon's *The Origins of Totalitarian Democracy* (1952) and *Political Messianism: the Romantic Phase* (1960). We do well to note that not until after the Second World War in the 1950-60 decade did any British-born-and-reared author venture to dip his feet in the chill waters of social and political ideologies, except Collingwood in 1942 (wondering what our war aims exactly were). So I turn to Britain.

CENTRALISED ÉTATISME

There was really only one political ideology that was *growing* throughout the last century, and so far throughout this, in Britain. It was that of centralised Statism and (later) Marxism, adopted and expounded first by the Radicals on the Left of the Liberals (who succeeded the Whigs); then—after the foundation of the Labour Group in Parliament in February 1900—by the Labour Party. The famous 'Clause IV' of the Labour Party encapsulated the ideology for the socialist Utopia: 'nationalisation of *all* the means of production, distribution, and exchange'; or, in so many words, monolithic central ownership and state control of the entire national economy. Orwell rightly saw where this led in his *1984* (drafted in wartime).

What part did economic ideas play in launching the Labour Party? The twin roots of the Labour Party were split from before its foundation: one root was the Christian (Puritanical) religion, Nonconformist mainly, though the Rev. F. D. Maurice was C. of E., like Tawney; the other root was severely laical, secular and (later) Marxist, following 'laics' like Adam Smith, Ricardo, the Mills, Jevons. This split dogged the Labour Party *ab initio*, re-opening in every major crisis: 1912, 1919-23, 1929-31, 1951 and 1981.

In the unfairly-termed 'stupid Party' (the Conservatives) there never was any ideology, since there was scarcely at any time any coherent and discernible set of political or programmatical principles. Typically British, Tories were 'agin' but seldom 'pro'. The Tories began last century by opposing the Whigs and went on doing so until Tory policies and programmes came to consist overwhelmingly of 'dishing the Whigs' or 'stealing their clothes while they were bathing'. The Tories went on that way this century—but against the Labour Party. They early foresaw—as the Liberal fifth Earl of Rosebery, Gladstone's Foreign Secretary and successor as Prime Minister in 1894-95 had foreseen—that the Liberal Party would be annihilated as an alternative Government by the onrush of the Socialist ideological advance in the hands of the Labour Party. From the late 1920s until 1979—half a century—Tory 'policy' was to 'dish the Socialists' by running an ever-expanding socialism better than the Labour Party could.

Should anyone think this my own idiosyncratic view, consider the following statement by that able Financial Secretary to the Treasury since 1979, Mr Nigel Lawson. He claimed that the 1979 Tory Government had begun a new course of 'peaceful counter-revolution':

'During the 25 years that followed Churchill it was a very

> different outlook that gained the intellectual ascendancy: the philosophy of social democracy, with its profound faith in the efficacy of government action, particularly in the economic sphere, and its deep commitment to the notion of "equality". To a greater or lesser extent the Conservative Party embraced both these delusions; the latter with some misgivings but fundamentally with a sense of resignation in the face of seeming historical inevitability; the former with little short of enthusiasm more based (in the economic sphere at least) in equal parts on a misreading of the economic lessons of the interwar years and a misunderstanding of Keynes.'[7]

(Did Mr Lawson really mean 'historical inevitability' (Marx) or merely intellectual dominance or fashion?)

The uninterrupted growth of Marxist ideology to eventual predominance in the British Labour *Movement*[8]—and lately almost to predominance in the local constituency parties and thus in the Parliamentary Labour Party—goes far to explain the absence of any overt, substantial, and significant Communist Party in Britain. This distinguishes Britain from France, Italy, the Low Countries, Spain, Scandinavia and almost all the other West European democracies except Western Germany and Eire. It also explains British socialism's wide breach from its Continental socialist brethren. A parliamentary Communist Party was not needed by Britain's communists and has long proved unnecessary. British socialism has steadily grown more Marxist for over a century—unlike the Continent's socialist parties. The devoted exponents of Marxist ideology have taken

[7] As reported in *The Times,* 5 August, 1980.

[8] Note: 'Movement' includes the Parliamentary Labour Party, all affiliated trade unions, *plus* local constituency parties, the Co-operative Party, etc.

it over (both its trade unions and its local constituency parties) from its Christian founders and its leaders last century and even up to 1945-51. The pro-socialist, pro-trade-union legislation of (first) Whig, then Liberal, then Tory governments has for long enfranchised, empowered, and even funded (by compulsory legal means) the trade unions and thus indirectly the Labour Movement and the Parliamentary Party. No other political party or movement in Britain has ever been, or is now, so legally privileged and safeguarded from the common law of the land.

IDEAS FOR ÉTATISME, NONE FOR ITS ALTERNATIVE

Dedicated Marxist ideologues and expositors had nearly controlled the Labour Party by the time of the General Strike in 1926. By 1931 the Party had openly split, part (at first) leading the 'National Government' coalition with Tories (and the diminishing Liberals) of that year; the other (Left-wing) part, sadly diminished, remaining independent. After participating in another coalition to conduct the Second World War in 1940, the massive Labour electoral victory of 1945 gave the Party sudden control of the complex, virtually totalitarian, economic and administrative apparatus which had run, and helped to win, that war, commanding two-thirds of the country's annual wartime output and resources.

This wartime structure proved a wonderful peacetime apparatus by which to build a socialist state. It was a time when, in admiration of Russian wartime efforts and sufferings, Marxist ideology could, and did, exert its peak appeal to a long-suffering British public, still severely rationed, seeking peaceful reconstruction, longing for realisation of Beveridge's 'Welfare State' (1944), and—once again—out to make 'a land fit for heroes' by state control over all housing, education, health, transport, coalmining, iron and steel and many other sectors of the economy, all of them candidates for 'nationalisation' by and for the socialist Welfare State. The Tories—and even less the vestigial Liberals—had no forward-looking, Heaven-on-earth Utopia to offer; nor, of course, any comforting and inspiring ideology.

There was widespread intellectual discontent, disagreement over governmental policies, and disillusion with *all* party politics in many intellectual quarters in the 1950s: among intellectual leaders of all party-political persuasions—to name but a few, Robbins, Hayek, Paish, Plant, Robertson, Hicks, and Colin Clark in the ranks of economists—but there was no focus for them, no intellectually congenial 'family forum', no meeting-place of like minds until around 1956 when the IEA was so modestly founded. It is interesting to wonder what might have happened in British politics, thought and development if from 1945 to 1956 the IEA had been in existence. From hindsight one can see that economists of the 'Left' (but on Labour's 'Right') like Durbin, Gaitskell, Gordon Walker, Jay and Crosland might well have shared thought and influence with Robbins and the others—and many more of that centre in politics (which the great American politician John C. Calhoun called 'the concurrent majority' between all parties) now so much in the news and in public comment.

Yet this socialist-Marxist euphoria evaporated in widespread disillusion under the post-war Labour governments in the late 1940s and in 1950-51. The abrupt ending of American 'lend-lease' supplies, the swiftly-aborted freeing of sterling in 1947, the first of so many post-war devaluations in 1949, the imaginative 'Marshall (later European Recovery) Plan' that gave all too little advantage to Britain, the painfully slow lifting of wartime controls, the all-too-gradual increasing of rations, the rapid economic recovery of other nations (especially ex-enemies)—all these ingredients of disillusion dispelled the hopes of victorious 1945. The British people returned the Tories to power in 1951 and kept them in power—almost unprecedentedly—until 1964, without their offering a vision of an alternative to *étatisme*.

But in that long run of Tory government the disillusion only deepened. It proved emphatically not enough for the Tories in the 1950s—and 1960s and 1970s—just to run a socialist Britain's Welfare State better than the socialists had done, or conceivably might do again. Despite (or was it *because* of?) expanding resources, growing tax revenues, more and more state expenditure on housing and education and 'health and welfare', and the eventual abolition of rationing—and despite (or *because* of?) conservation of the central and local governmental controls over private enterprises and of those forcibly turned into 'nationalised industries' by the socialists' ideology—disillusion, political scepticism and popular dismay became more widespread. It ended with the return of the Labour Party to power in 1964, this time inwardly strengthened in Marxist ideology. Even so the (by this time bewildered and bemused) British electorate only gave Labour a further six years. By 1970 the worst Conservative Government—the most ignorant, ineffectual and damaging since Neville Chamberlain's in the fatal run-up to 1939—had been returned, only to be ignominiously hounded out in 1974. Then, 'handy-dandy', Labour again, till 1979: by which time the dimensions of our national disaster were plain for all everywhere, at home and abroad, to see.

However, some had perceived such a disaster looming ahead in the 1950s—20 to 25 years earlier. From many of them came the inspiration and contributory effort that set up and energised the IEA in the mid-1950s and kept it going so successfully and convincingly thereafter.

IEA'S INTELLECTUAL ORIGINS

The two great inspirers of all who conceived, founded and contributed to the IEA were Hayek and his former colleague Robbins—both still happily with us. Each had a considerable following, almost a 'school'. Hayek from *The Road to Serfdom* (1944) went on to found the international, and increasingly influential, Mont Pélerin Society (1947). Robbins, after his war work, had especial influence in Britain, first among a batch of remarkably gifted economic and financial journalists; and later, perhaps, some in the rapidly multiplying economics faculties of the new institutions of higher learning (universities, polytechnics, colleges of advanced technology, etc.) as the outcome of the new Education Act and the 'Robbins' recommendations for higher education. One significant feature of British economic and financial journalism after the war is the growing number of once socialist writers who changed nearer to the standpoint and outlook of Hayek, Robbins, or others in the IEA: one thinks of Sam Brittan, Peter Jay, (the late) Patrick Hutber, Alan Day, John Vaizey, Ronald Butt, Paul Johnson, and many another, as the older ones may well think of Colin Clark (or me) nearly 50 years ago.

As the disappointments of the 1945-55 decade mounted and the end of 'Marshall Aid' (1952) loomed up, the (unanimous) reports of the 66 productivity teams of employers, trade unionists and professional experts which had visited the USA (to examine and report on Britain's post-war problems and inefficiencies compared with American experience and methods) had stirred up national concern for Britain's economic future. That concern, shared by trade union leaders and politicians of all parties, culminated in the publication of my *We Too Can Prosper: the Promise of Productivity* (Allen & Unwin, 1953), and in the campaign all over the country of the British (formerly the Anglo-American) Productivity Council with its local committees. This concern with productivity in individual works and localities involved much detailed 'micro-economic' work. It accompanied public anxiety about our national future and for the new young Queen. It accompanied growing concern among the fast-diminishing band of admirable trade union leaders (Bevin, Deakin, Carron, Williamson, Lincoln Evans, Tanner, etc.) and among many newer and younger MPs and journalists of all political parties.

THIRTY YEARS OF CRISIS

The disappointment and disillusion were all the more bitter by the 1950s, and went all the deeper, because inordinately high hopes of more welfare under a more dynamic, more equitable and more productive society had been encouraged by socialist claims for the newly nationalised, newly 'socialised' fuel, transport and steel industries and health and other welfare services formerly under private ownership and direction. More and more state control was socialists' cardinal belief for making society 'better'. (It still is.) On the contrary: productivity and quality in British industrial production and in public services alike, and industrial relations in *both* sectors, steadily deteriorated, accompanied by wilder and wilder pay claims, ever more frequent and damaging strikes, and (inevitably) accelerating inflation.[9] In very different circumstances from those of pre-war days, Tory governments after 1951, obsessed by macro-measures, fell back on Keynesian reflationary policies of the 1920s and 1930s when Mr Harold Macmillan (Prime Minister from 1957 to 1963) had written, from his experience in those earlier days, *Reconstruction: A Plea for a National Policy* (1933), *Planning for Employment* (1935), *The Next Five Years* (1935) and (most significant) *The Middle Way* (1938, re-issued 1966)—a middle way to an 'everlasting bonfire'. No wonder people talked of 'Butskellism', Butler+Gaitskell-ism. Why were they thus obsessed? Why were Robbins and Hayek *et al.,* so blatantly ignored, derided even? Here we can only repeat the German soldier's admonition from the First World War: *Nicht ärgern, nur wundern!* ('Don't be bitter about it, just wonder'). The brilliant band of international perceivers listed above saw from 1900 onwards—even before—whither the mass-collectivism, mass-demagogical publicity, aiming at centralised monolithic power, masquerading as 'inevitable' destiny, was bound to lead

[9] Graham Hutton, *Inflation and Society*, Allen & Unwin, 1960.

even the best-intentioned of men, most of whom turned out in the course of events to be the easiest to confuse, 'con' and captivate. But *why* so many intellectuals followed such dubious leaders is a profound problem.

Hugh Gaitskell, Chancellor of the Exchequer, foreseeing the slippery slope being created by overmanning, overspending and over-pay, could say in the Commons as early as 10 April 1951:[10]

> 'I must draw the attention of the Committee and of the country to a real danger which, because we in this country have in the past successfully avoided it, is often ignored; the danger that, if incomes and prices rise swiftly or continuously, there may be a progressive loss of confidence in the value of money. Were such confidence to be lost we should be plunged into inflation of the most violent kind, which in other countries has on more than one occasion brought the whole fabric of their social and political life to the edge of disaster.'

Not much has changed in the British economic crisis and the debates over it in the last 30 years.

Gaitskell's concern was shared, before and after, by many Labour colleagues uncontaminated by ideology. Among them were two whose books had much influence: Anthony Crosland's *The Future of Socialism* (Cape, 1956) and Douglas Jay's *Socialism in the New Society* (Longmans, 1961). Even the ideological 'Dick' Crossman had to confess to disillusionment with Marxist ideology and practice—and, with his socialist fellow-contributors, to fears for liberty under socialism—in their essays *The God That Failed* (Hamilton, 1950). A group of Liberal writers concerned for liberties under the new Socialism and the Welfare State was also

[10] *Hansard*, House of Commons, Vol. 486, no. 83, col. 840.

at work in the 1950s and published a set of essays (Allen & Unwin, 1957) under the title *The Unservile State*. The 1950s were indeed a decade of political and intellectual ferment, a period of old clashing with new ideas and of initiatives with reactions. The mood of national self-questioning was summarised by an anonymous and critical 'front' article in *The Times Literary Supplement* of 24 February 1956,[11] comparing British national economic performance, and British prospects, with others. Entitled *The Dynamic Society* (simultaneously issued as a pamphlet), it went to all Cabinet Ministers and a wider circle of public figures. Its title passed into the common cant of British public affairs. It makes sad reading today, 25 years later.

THE REVOLUTION OF THE IEA

Nevertheless the advent of the IEA and its functions as forum and intellectual power-house clearly worked a ferment in both economic and politico-social thinking in Britain, and acceleratingly throughout the 1960s and 1970s. Both in academic economics and in national (all-party) politics the challenge of the Institute's writers to the post-war crudely Keynesian economics and policy-making—which Keynes would have disowned—worked what must be termed a revolution. Against the fashionably crude Keynesianism of 1945 to 1970 arose an increasingly respectable, increasingly intellectually esteemed, and at length almost fashionable body of economic and socio-political thought, querying *étatisme*, state-interventionism, monolithic centralism, and the false gods of crude Keynesianism, as well as expounding and analysing the rôle of the freest possible market

[11] [The author was the writer of this Chapter.—ED.]

system on both the *macro* and *micro* scales. Around no other significant focus or forum did such an intellectual movement revolve. It was a remarkable achievement, obviously meeting a long-existent though muted and long-ignored need.

So strong has been the swing away from the post-war pseudo-Keynesian *étatisme* and economic thinking that both in the Labour and Tory parties, and in their intellectual 'think-tanks', the formerly fashionable pseudo-Keynesians are by now manifestly on the defensive, and—as in America and even in Eastern Europe—the freeing of markets as a guarantee of individual liberties and more material welfare has become both arguable and pursuable, both as means and as an end. That this movement took shape first at the IEA in Britain is much to the credit of its first begetters, and then of its swiftly-multiplying authors and other associates and supporters.

Such are but a few signs of the ferment out of which was precipitated the IEA, which became the haven for refugees from all parties and from none, calling on the thinking—and re-thinking—of scores of economists, young and not-so-young, little known and world-renowned, and upon which in turn it was increasingly to exert its influence. By 1957 the time was over-ripe for a return to realism—from Utopianism and ideology to reason and reality, from macro-fancies to micro-facts.

Chapter II

THE CHANGING INTELLECTUAL CLIMATE IN ECONOMICS

T. W. Hutchison

Professor of Economics,
University of Birmingham

The Author

TERENCE W. HUTCHISON is Professor of Economics at the University of Birmingham. Before the war he taught in Bonn and Baghdad, and served in the Indian Army Intelligence, 1941-46, attached to the Government of India 1945-46.

He was a Lecturer (1947-51) and Reader (1951-56) at the London School of Economics, Visiting Professor at Columbia University 1954-55, Visiting Fellow at the University of Saarbrücken 1962. Visiting Professor at Yale University, 1963-64, Visiting Fellow at Australian National University, Canberra, 1967, and Visiting Professor at Dalhousie University, Halifax, Nova Scotia, 1970, Keio University, Tokyo, 1973, and the University of Western Australia, 1975.

He is the author of numerous works, including three IEA Papers—the last one being *Keynes v. the 'Keynesians' . . .?* (Hobart Paperback 10, 1977)—and *Revolution and Progress in Economic Knowledge* (Cambridge University Press, 1978). Professor Hutchison is a member of the IEA's Advisory Council.

The Changing Intellectual Climate in Economics

I. WHEN DID IT ALL START TO GO WRONG?

When did it all start to go wrong? Some authorities (like Mr Christopher Booker, for example)[1] try to trace the errors of our time back to certain hubristic presumptions of the Renaissance and the Enlightenment regarding an illusory human capacity for managing, or planning, man's future, on the assumption of his perfectibility. Others, with 'environmental' anxieties, go back to 'the Industrial Revolution'. Others, again, might go back to Adam and Eve.

We are not attempting here such cosmic perspectives. We shall eventually come to focus on the decade of the 1950s, when the IEA was being conceived and launched, that is, not so much on the Garden of Eden as on the premierships of Sir Anthony Eden and his immediate predecessor, Churchill, and successor, Macmillan. Our argument will be largely concerned with the question why 'the intellectual climate' precluded, before that decade, a successful deployment and penetration of opinion in Britain of free market ideas; or, in other words, why an effective and successful IEA was not

[1] *The Seventies: The Decade That Changed The Future*, Stein & Day, New York, 1980, Part I ('The Death of Progress'), Chapter 3.

likely to have come into existence before the 1950s. Of course, the torch of market ideas could be, and was, kept burning, and important prophetic pronouncements—like Hayek's *Road to Serfdom*, written in wartime Britain and published in 1944—were recorded. But, in the well-known words of J. S. Mill, ideas 'have in general no very rapid or immediate efficacy in human affairs', *except when 'outward circumstances conspire' with them*. Our argument is that, in Britain, it was only in the 1950s that 'outward circumstances' began sufficiently to 'conspire' for the successful emergence of the IEA.

But we must certainly start quite a long way back, at that turning-point in British—and, to some extent world-wide—politico-economic history which took place around 1870, and which was to some extent connected with the major turning-point in the history of economic thought in Britain at about that date.

II. THE ENGLISH CLASSICAL MARKET ECONOMY

The English classical free-market economy came to its full development in the middle third of the 19th century and reached the apogee of its success around 1860, with Britain far and away the leading economic and industrial power, justifiably renowned as 'the workshop of the world'. It was in the course of the 1860s that free market principles, or the idea (as Mill put it) of '*laissez-faire* the general rule', began to lose their hold. We would follow Professor E. J. Hobsbawm in taking 'around 1860' as marking 'the peak of British *laissez-*

faire', of which, he maintains, 'the foundations crumbled in the 1860s and 1870s'.[2] Why did this crumbling begin at a time of, or so soon following, such apparently overwhelming and unique success?

It is surely important for those concerned with the revival of free market ideas and policies in Britain to recognise what was the political basis of the classical market economy, in the middle of the 19th century in this country, when such ideas and policies were at the peak of their prestige and influence; as well as to realise just why they proved, so soon afterwards, so vulnerable to the long process of erosion and supersession over the ensuing 100 years.

The framework of English classical market economy had been completed in the 1830s and 1840s, in particular, by the reforms of the Poor Law (1834), the Bank of England (1844), and the Corn Laws (1846). These reforms were put through on the basis of the electorate established by the Reform Bill of 1832, which consisted, roughly, of about the 15 per cent wealthiest, property-owning males in the population.[3] That was the political basis on which the classical market economy was completed, and on which it operated in its halcyon days of the 1850s and early 1860s.

It seems, therefore, that the Marxian model, based on Engels' acute observation of Manchester in the early 1840s, was not essentially, or extremely, at fault regarding what might be called the 'power-structure' of

[2] *Industry and Empire,* Pelican edn., Penguin Books, 1969, p. 96.

[3] A fuller exposition of the argument here is in the author's IEA Occasional Paper 10, *Markets and the Franchise* (1966), to be republished in a much revised form in *The Politics and Philosophy of Economics,* Blackwell, Oxford, 1981.

British 'capitalism', or its politico-economic framework, in that phase of its history. The young Disraeli, at almost exactly the same juncture as Engels, described 'the two nations' in Britain in closely similar terms to those of Engels.[4] Whether or not the 'proletarians', in this country, had 'nothing to lose but their chains', the vast majority of people, at the lower reaches of the income pyramid, were unprotected constitutionally by political power: they possessed no vote and were mostly equipped with little or no union power. There seems very little reason to suppose that Adam Smith would not have continued to hold, as he had insisted three-quarters of a century earlier, that power in the labour market, in Britain, was generally tilted quite heavily in favour of 'the masters'.[5]

[4] *Sybil, or the Two Nations*, 1845, especially Book II, Chapter 5, and the descriptions of 'Wodgate' in Book III, Chapter 4.

[5] 'We rarely hear, it has been said, of the combinations of masters; though frequently of those of workmen. But whoever imagines, upon this account, that masters rarely combine, is as ignorant of the world as of the subject. Masters are always and every where in a sort of tacit, but constant and uniform combination, not to raise the wages of labour above their actual rate. . . .
Such combinations, however, are frequently resisted by a contrary defensive combination of the workmen; who sometimes too, without any provocation of this kind, combine of their own accord to raise the price of their labour. . . . In order to bring the point to a speedy decision, they have always recourse to the loudest clamour, and sometimes to the most shocking violence and outrage. They are desperate, and act with the folly and extravagance of desperate men, who must either starve, or frighten their masters into an immediate compliance with their demands.
The masters upon these occasions are just as clamorous upon the other side, and never cease to call aloud for the assistance of the civil magistrate, and the rigorous execution of those

[*Continued opposite*]

III. THE POLITICAL FRAMEWORK OF MARKETS IN BRITAIN AND THE USA

A vast and heavily consequential contrast must be recognised between the emergence and early history of the market economy in Britain, as compared with the United States. Regarding the market economy in the US it has recently been argued:

> 'At the beginning of the nineteenth century, the natural rights justification for property was entirely compatible with a decentralised market economy. Under these circumstances, it was still possible to believe that those who engaged in market transactions possessed relatively equal bargaining power and that the results of the market system would produce a reliable distribution of rewards according to the ability and energy of those who participated. Indeed, the market was thought to be the most

laws which have been enacted with so much severity against the combinations of servants, labourers, and journeymen. The workmen, accordingly, very seldom derive any advantage from the violence of those tumultuous combinations, which, partly from the interposition of the civil magistrate, partly from the superior steadiness of the masters, partly from the necessity which the greater part of the workmen are under of submitting for the sake of present subsistence, generally end in nothing, but the punishment or ruin of the ringleaders. . . .

In disputes with their workmen masters must generally have the advantage.' (*The Wealth of Nations*, Modern Library edition, ed. Cannan, pp. 66-7.) Smith's description of labour markets in his day differs somewhat from economic theorists' descriptions of competitive markets. Professor W. H. Hutt (*The Theory of Collective Bargaining 1930-1975*, Hobart Paperback 8, IEA, 1975, pp. 23-25) holds that Adam Smith was wrong. We would not go quite so far as those who maintain that Adam Smith was *never* wrong. But Professor Hutt does not seem to have provided strong evidence that Smith was wrong regarding the above-quoted description of labour markets in his day.

> powerful institutional expression of the ideal of equality of opportunity.'[6]

On the other hand, it could not conceivably be maintained, at the beginning of the 19th century, or probably at any time in that century in Britain, that the market economy, as it then operated, could be thought of as 'the most powerful institutional expression of the ideal of equality of opportunity', as it had actually been created on the basis of Disraeli's two nations—not to mention its approximation, in the 1840s, to the Marxian model.

MARKET ECONOMY AND INEQUALITY IN BRITAIN . . .

Indeed, the market economy in Britain was launched on the basis of a degree of inherited political and economic inequality to which there was no parallel among white Americans, and which was also quite non-comparable with the inequalities remaining in Britain a century later. Many, or most, English economists who have pronounced on the principles of economic policy during the last 100 years or so have certainly seemed to hold that such vast inherited inequalities must be taken into account in their views regarding taxation and, indeed, the rôle of government. Indeed, insofar as what J. S. Mill called a society based on 'the principle of private property' may be equated with the market economy, he amply confirmed, at the very height of its success in Britain, the comparison we are drawing:

[6] M. J. Horowitz, 'The Legacy of 1776 in Legal and Economic Thought', *Journal of Law and Economics,* Vol. XIX (3), October 1976, p. 629.

'The principle of private property has never yet had a fair trial in any country; and less so perhaps in this country than in some others. The social arrangements of modern Europe commenced from a distribution of property which was the result, not of just partition, or acquisition by industry, but of conquest and violence; and notwithstanding what industry has been doing for many centuries to modify the work of force, the system still retains many and large traces of its origin.

The laws of property have never yet conformed to the principles on which the justification of private property rests. They have made property of things which never ought to be property, and absolute property where only a qualified property ought to exist. They have not held the balance fairly between human beings, but have heaped impediments on some, to give advantages to others; they have purposely fostered inequalities, and prevented all starting fair in the race.

That all should indeed start on perfectly equal terms is inconsistent with any law of private property: but if as much pains as has been taken to aggravate the inequality of chances arising from the natural working of the principle, had been taken to temper that inequality by every means not subversive of that principle itself; if the tendency of legislation had been to favour the diffusion, instead of the concentration of wealth . . . the principle of individual property would have been found to have no necessary connection with the physical and social evils which almost all Socialist writers assume to be inseparable from it.'[7]

. . . BUT NOT IN THE USA

Certainly in the United States vast inherited inequalities began to emerge in due course. But, among the

[7] *Principles of Political Economy* (1848), ed. Ashley, 1909, II, 1, 3.

white population, they were not nearly so massively built-in from the very start as in Europe. (Indeed, of course, to get out from under the vast inherited European inequalities was often, presumably, an important motive for crossing the Atlantic.)

Some American libertarians, and other free market economists, have tended to regard leading English neo-classicals who, in the half-century after 1870, advocated various extensions of the rôle of government, and progressive taxation to finance them, as having, more or less seriously, 'sold the pass' as regards liberty, or as having more or less betrayed market principles in urging policy in Britain towards a 'mixed economy'.

In some cases, in recent decades, these criticisms may be to some extent justified. (Certainly they are far less wide of the mark than grotesque condemnations of the same 'neo-classicals' for advocating *laissez-faire* in as extreme, or even more extreme, terms than the classicals.)[8] But such strictures are not justified to the extent that they leave out of account the scale of the initial, inherited political and economic inequalities which in Britain, as contrasted with the United States, were initially built into the market economy, and which it retained through its great period of success.

[8] Professor Joan Robinson: 'For fifty years before 1914 the established economists of various schools had all been preaching one doctrine, with great self-confidence, and pomposity—the doctrine of *laissez-faire*'. ('The Second Crisis of Economic Theory', *American Economic Review: Papers and Proceedings*, May 1972, p. 2). Also Phyllis Deane, *The Evolution of Economic Ideas*, Cambridge University Press, 1978, p. 101: 'The neo-classical economists were able to retain unimpaired the classical bias towards economic individualism and *laissez-faire*'.

IV. THE LONG DECLINE AND FALL OF THE CLASSICAL MARKET ECONOMY

It was following the Reform Bill of 1867—coincidentally the year in which Marx published Volume I of *Capital*—that Britain set off on the long ineluctable erosion of the classical free-market economy (which was accompanied, of course, by the ever-increasing institutional obsolescence, in the first 'capitalist' country, of the Marxian politico-economic model).[9] The reform came as a stroke of political entrepreneurial opportunism by Disraeli, and was specially concerned with angling—by both Disraeli and Gladstone—for the support of the newly enfranchised artisan, the 'aristocracy of labour', with its craft unions.

Anyhow, there followed immediately the Acts of 1871 and 1875 laying the foundations of trade union power in this country.[10] The 1867 Reform not only brought a highly consequential shift in electoral power, but also presaged further inevitable shifts in the same direction, which duly came, in the first instance in 1884, with another major extension of the franchise to the less well-off. J. S. Mill supported the 1867 reform, as, on the whole, did Jevons, his theoretical opponent. Jevons, the leading initiator in Britain of the today widely castigated 'neo-classical economics', was also representative of the fundamental change in climate regarding econ-

[9] Another great modern work of political economy which almost from the year it was published began also to suffer seriously from the increasing institutional obsolescence of its general model was Keynes's *General Theory* (Macmillan, 1936).

[10] See also on this development the author's IEA Occasional Paper 10, *Markets and the Franchise*, cited above (footnote 3, p. 23).

omic policy doctrines in this period. As Professor Hayek has put it:

> 'The end of the liberal era of principles might well be dated at the time when . . . W. S. Jevons pronounced that in economic and social policy, "we can lay down no hard and fast rules but must treat every case upon its merits".'[11]

MISGIVINGS ABOUT ECONOMIC CONSEQUENCES OF 1867 ACT

Whiggish and Conservative opponents of the 1867 Reform were quite clear about the implications for economic policies. As Lord Salisbury saw the prospects, when the franchise was extended to the poorer majority:

> 'The rich would pay all the taxes and the poor make all the laws . . .
> The bestowal on any class of a voting power disproportionate to their stake in the country must infallibly give to that class a power *pro tanto* of using taxation as an instrument of plunder, and expenditure and legislation as a fountain of gain.'[12]

Lord Salisbury was observing, in other words, that, for a kind of politico-economic equilibrium to be reached, the distribution of wealth, or of 'stakes in the country', must be proportionate to voting power (which, of course, in some conditions of universal suffrage would imply egalitarianism). Anyhow, significant shifts in economic policy objectives, and in ideas

[11] *Law, Legislation and Liberty*, Routledge & Kegan Paul, Vol. I, 1973, p. 59.

[12] Quoted in G. Cecil, *Life of Robert, Marquis of Salisbury*, Hodder & Stoughton, 1921, Vol. I, pp. 149 and 153.

about the rôle and responsibilities of government, soon began to emerge, especially after the extension of 1884. On the one hand, leading political entrepreneurs, like Joseph Chamberlain, with his 'Radical Programme' of 1885, began to advocate progressive taxation to pay for 'social reforms'. On the other hand, leading academic economists—and most of the leading economists were now academics—began to develop arguments for progressive taxation, as against the classical doctrine of, in the main, proportionality. Economists were also taking increasingly much more seriously the problems of cyclical instability, and irregularity of employment, as causes of poverty, which had not generally been regarded as very serious problems by the leading classicals.[13]

MARSHALL AND 'THE PROBLEM OF POVERTY'

It was to this fundamental change in climate that Alfred Marshall was responding when he announced in 1893 that for the previous 25 years, that is virtually from the start of his work as an economist, he had devoted himself to 'the problem of poverty', and that 'very little of my work has been devoted to any enquiry which does not bear on that'.[14] Let it be emphasised at once that Marshall's poverty problem was one of absolute and not simply of 'relative poverty'. But it might be maintained that Smith, Ricardo, and J. S. Mill had been

[13] Professor P. Schwartz, regarding J. S. Mill, for example, has emphasised the 'assumption underlying all his work, namely the impossibility of prolonged involuntary unemployment'. (*The New Political Economy of J. S. Mill*, Duke, North Carolina, 1972, p. 38.)

[14] Marshall, *Official Papers*, Macmillan, 1926, p. 205.

just as centrally concerned with 'the problem of poverty' as Marshall. There is, however, a vital and profound contrast. The implication of *The Wealth of Nations* is that poverty is to be dealt with, simply or primarily, by seeking to promote the growth in the wealth of the nation, or by endeavouring to keep it in a progressive state, with wages above the natural level. Beyond that, for Adam Smith, there is very little to be said about poverty, except that, in any case, there will be, eventually, 'natural' limits to its alleviation. For Ricardo and J. S. Mill, as upholders of pretty hard-line views about population and wages, these natural limits, certainly in any short or medium term, were more definitely and tightly drawn.

Nor, as already noted, was unemployment or instability regarded as a fundamentally serious problem by the leading classicals. Marshall probably retained a more cautious concern for classical reservations about the alleviation of poverty, and tended to regard the unemployment problem as less serious, than his leading contemporaries and successors, such as Edgeworth, Foxwell, Cannan or Pigou. But he emphasised the depth of the contrast with his classical predecessors. Of the 'doctrines that were universal among the economists of the beginning of the century', and were 'fairly true in their time', Marshall stated:

> 'The doctrine is that if you tax the rich, and give money to the working classes, the result will be that the working classes will increase in number, and the result will be that you will have lowered wages in the next generation; and the grant will not have improved the position of the working classes on the whole. As regards this *a change has come, which separates the economics of this generation*

from the economics of the past; . . . That change insists upon the fact that if the money is so spent as to increase the earning power of the next generation, it may not lower wages.'[15]

Anyhow, Marshall went along with progressive taxation and the 1909 Budget of Lloyd George, while earlier he had given cautious approval to Joseph Chamberlain's proposals for relief works for the unemployed (1886).

THE NEO-CLASSICALS' CONCERN ABOUT POVERTY AND UNEMPLOYMENT

Other 'neo-classicals' of this time, in their concern with 'the problem of poverty', argued, on the one hand, like Edgeworth and Cannan, for progressive taxation; while Foxwell insisted (1886) that 'uncertainty of employment is the root evil of the present industrial régime'. Later the young Pigou went much further in both these directions. In particular, because of the 'uncertainty of employment' and the poverty which it caused, increasing attention came to be paid to the problem of cyclical fluctuations. Certainly the English 'neo-classicals' had mostly been rather behind the

[15] *Official Papers, op. cit.*, p. 225 (italics added). It may be noted that Marshall was highly critical of universal government pensions: Universal pensions '. . . do not contain, in themselves, the seeds of their own disappearance. I am afraid that, if started, they would tend to become perpetual. I regard all this problem of poverty as a passing evil in the progress of man upwards; and I should not like any institution started which did not contain in itself the causes which would make it shrivel up as the causes of poverty itself shrivelled up'. (Evidence to the *Royal Commission on the Aged Poor*, 1893, *Official Papers, op. cit.*, p. 244.) I am very grateful to Arthur Seldon for calling my attention to this passage.

leading Continental writers on this problem, most of whom had come under the influence either of Marx or of the German Historical School. But by 1914, as Dr Jose Harris, in her authoritative study of unemployment and politics in Britain, has observed:

> '. . . fatalistic acceptance of the inevitability of the trade cycle and doctrinaire prejudice against the relief of unemployment had largely passed away.'[16]

Thus in less than half a century since the 1867 reform, and following what has been called 'the Jevonian revolution', the economic order in Britain, and the principles of economic policy, had been transformed as compared with those of the English classical model. The powers of trade unions, progressive taxation, and elementary social services had been well established and the case for policies against unemployment widely recognised.

There is, however, one further, in some ways contrasting, achievement for which the leading neo-classicals may be ascribed some responsibility—insofar as economists ever can be ascribed responsibility for policy. The campaign for tariffs, waged from 1903 by Joseph Chamberlain, was defeated, though only for another quarter of a century; and Marshall, Pigou, and other neo-classical economists played a part in that pre-war victory of free trade.

[16] J. Harris, *Unemployment and Politics: A Study in English Social Policy 1886-1914*, Oxford University Press, 1972, p. 5.

V. TOWARDS THE 'MIXED' ECONOMY

Perhaps today some (or many) libertarians would not, in retrospect, condemn the kind of policy changes carried through, in the main, with the support of leading English neo-classical economists, in the decades before 1914. Certainly it does not seem that the English classical market economy could have survived, with its pristine freedom and competitiveness, *unless* the electoral reforms of 1867 and 1884 had been blocked—in which case the Marxian model had, not implausibly, predicted revolution.

The question remains how far the demands of the new electorate could have been met in ways which did not ultimately lead on to the eventual widespread supersession, or paralysing, of market mechanisms in the course of the next century. How far, that is, could Marshall's 'problem of poverty' have been adequately treated in ways which met the demands of the new voters, but which, at the same time, were market-supportive rather than market-frustrating?

For example, could, *first*, the balance in the labour market have been rendered rather less unfavourable to labour, without incurring, or risking, that it would eventually be tilted right down on the other side? *Second*, how far could the causes of poverty have been remedied without the inevitable emergence of the kind of tax levels, and the vast health and educational bureaucracies for whose benefit our social services are largely run today? *Third*, how far (under the gold standard in the first instance) could the problems of instability and unemployment, regarded increasingly seriously by leading neo-classicals, have been alleviated without eventual dangers of chronic inflation, bearing in mind the increasing involvement of democratic government, or what Sir John Hicks has called 'the nationalisation of money'?

Of course, such questions are practically unanswerable. But it seems very difficult to feel confident that fully affirmative answers could in practice have been forthcoming, in the circumstances of the time. (Economists are not only reluctant sometimes to proclaim their ignorance about how to deal with the problems of their day; they seem apt to claim that *answers were always there, and must have been there,* for the problems of the past.) But, with hindsight, it seems that a preponderance of regulative paternalism in the infant 'social services' may well have been almost inevitable. Could, for example, additional tax-revenue have been elicited from the tax-payers of the day, to finance freedom of choice in health and education services for the inhabitants of 'Wodgate', as depicted by Disraeli, or for the underworld of Mayhew's London? Could voucher schemes have been used in order to 'induce', in Robert Lowe's terms, 'our future masters to learn their letters'?[17] Or would the climate of influential opinion at that time have excluded such a latter-day, libertarian idea as then, politically, completely unrealistic?

Doubtless economists should have been much more concerned than they were to explore market-supportive arrangements, and to emphasise libertarian principles. But it may be indulging in a kind of rather pretentious,

[17] As W. E. Forster, who carried through the 1870 Education Act, paternalistically maintained: 'We have to deal with weak people; we have to deal with people who themselves have to deal with strong people, who are borne down, who are tempted, who are unfortunate in the circumstances of life'.

hind-sighted over-optimism to suppose that, in the climate of the day, the rates of taxation and the freedoms of the pre-1867 classical market economy could have been preserved.

UNIVERSAL SUFFRAGE, 'MIXED' ECONOMY AND EROSION OF INDIVIDUAL LIBERTY

The long movement towards a 'mixed' economy got under way in Britain because, in response to the new demands of the wider electorate, a more 'mixed' range of policy objectives came to be adopted, requiring higher levels of taxation and an extension of the duties of government. To a large extent the new policy objectives were competitive rather than complementary with the old, that is, the reduction of inequalities and insecurities conflicted, at the margin, with the preservation of the old liberties. In practice, the change was so profound and far-reaching as to bring about the sole successful emergence of an (eventually) new party of government, in the modern history of party politics in Britain. Of course, such conflicts of objectives are rejected by those who regard one single objective—liberty, or 'welfare'—as a kind of single, absolute maximand. But the neo-classical economists who supported, or went along with, the early moves towards the mixed economy might have formulated the political philosophy, and pluralist objectives, by which they were guided in the words of Edmund Burke:

> 'It is besides a very great mistake to imagine, that mankind follow up practically any speculative principle, either of government or of freedom, as far as it will go in argument and logical distillation. We Englishmen stop very short of the principles upon which we support any

given part of our constitution; or even the whole of it together. . . . This is nothing but what is natural and proper. All government, indeed every human benefit and enjoyment, every virtue, and every prudent act, is founded on compromise and barter. We balance inconveniences; we give and take; we remit some rights, that we may enjoy others; and we choose rather to be happy citizens, than subtle disputants. As we must give away some natural liberty, to enjoy civil advantages; so we must sacrifice some civil liberties, for the advantages to be derived from the communion and fellowship of a great empire.'[18]

VI. 1914-1945

We have dealt at some length with the period down to 1914 because this was when the foundations were laid, the vital first steps undertaken, and the long trend established in Britain of the ever-extending rôle of government in the economy—sometimes rather pretentiously described as 'Wagner's Law' (that government expenditure will grow faster than national income). In economically more advanced countries, over the last century, with one outstanding exception (to be mentioned below), this trend has continued relentlessly. Obviously two world wars immensely accelerated the trend, with post-war cut-backs never reducing government expenditure and activity to the pre-war levels.

The 31 years from 1914 to 1945 were a period of continuous, fundamental upheaval and disequilibrium, with World War I, Post-War, Great Slump, Pre-War II,

[18] *The Works of Edmund Burke,* World's Classics edition, Vol. II, 1906, p. 226.

and World War II, following one another with only brief, fleeting lulls in the storm. (Incidentally, with the addition of six years before World War I, these 31 years made up Keynes's career as an economist.)

WORLD WAR AND THE ADVENT OF 'TOTAL ECONOMIC PLANNING'

The First World War began in Britain with an attempt at 'Business as Usual' (in Churchill's phrase), as had been more or less possible for this country in previous wars before the 20th century. But as the conflict continued, Britain muddled—or was bit-by-bit forced—into total economic planning for total war, which came to be regarded as essential for victory. Again, at the outbreak of the Second World War, Professor Hayek urged that market mechanisms should be used for allocating materials, and the interest rate for allocating investments.[19] But in view of the huge uncertainties involved, it does not seem very surprising that in the economically simplified conditions of wartime such mechanisms were not regarded as acting with sufficient guaranteed rapidity, with Hitler at the gates. So total

[19] 'Pricing versus Rationing' and 'The Economy of Capital', in *The Banker*, September and October 1939, pp. 242 ff and 38 ff. Professor Hayek posed the question for the war-time economy: 'Should we rely on the price mechanism to provide us with an indicator of the relative scarcity of the various factors of production? Or should we deliberately make this price mechanism inoperative and try to substitute for it a detailed regulation of all productive activity by a central authority? And the argument that the rate of interest should be allowed to express the real scarcity of capital is fundamentally the same as that with respect to any other price' (*op. cit.*, p. 39). See also the comments of T. C. Koopmans, *Three Essays on the State of Economic Science*, McGraw Hill, 1968, p. 146.

economic planning, widely held to have been successful in having brought victory in the first war, was re-deployed, in some ways more effectively, in the second.

Moreover, war conditions brought not only something close to total planning, but, almost inevitably, major central regulations promoting egalitarianism, or at least the reduction of inequalities under near-siege conditions. Some kinds of controls and price-fixing, like rent controls, survived the wars with highly deleterious, long-term, market-frustrating effects. Though after World War I there was a powerful urge to get back to the normality (or 'normalcy') of pre-1914, the operation of 'Wagner's Law' left taxation much higher and social services much more fully developed. Even more significant perhaps for the market economy was the undermining of the British and world monetary framework and the greatly increased power of the trade unions.

As we have seen, most of these trends—apart from the undermining of the monetary framework—were firmly and clearly established in Britain well before 1914. But certainly, after the war, unemployment, for which there were now regular official statistics, emerged at a much higher rate (as Keynes found when he first turned to the problem in 1924, and recommended closely similar measures to those he was to support through all the strenuous theoretical developments of the following decades). Indeed, Keynes can be regarded as taking up the British unemployment problem just where the Webbs, Beveridge and Pigou had left it before 1914.

WAS RETURN TO GOLD STANDARD 'A FATAL DECISION'?

An extremely important rôle in the emergence of the unemployment problem in Britain, and in the development of British phobias regarding deflation—and hence of vital elements in Keynesian economics—has been ascribed to the return to the gold standard at the former parity in 1925. This seems to have been represented as a fatal decision, the avoidance of which would have warded off the worst of what followed. But the significance of the alternative, that is, the abandonment of the previous parity, must also be weighed in the balance—as it was at the time by Pigou. A parity change would have constituted an abandonment of the central, 'natural' gold-standard principle, and the suggestion of moveable parities, with its effects on expectations, would also have had profound long-run consequences and would have given ground to the encroachments of political management. A readiness to face the fundamental adjustments required for the British economy would hardly have been encouraged. Replacing the gold standard, after its long prestigious reign, with democratically elected governments exercising, or claiming, increasing influence, was bound to bring a phase of fundamental disequilibrium.

Meanwhile, apart from the war-time decades, the 'thirties were surely the most politically crisis-ridden decade of this century, with deflation and unemployment assisting immensely the rise of Nazism. The climate, indeed, could hardly have been more unfavourable for the effective working of market mechanisms or for their advocacy by economists in some anticipation of the IEA.

VII. POST-WAR II

We traced earlier how the shift of power, brought about by the extensions of the franchise in the last third of the 19th century, led to new policy demands posing new problems for economic policy and for economists concerned with the real world. Also of great importance for the climate of opinion, in promoting or excluding different kinds of policies, are the recent economic histories and experiences of different countries, and the ways they are interpreted.

BRITAIN AND GERMANY: CONTRAST IN POLICY AND RESULTS

The economic achievements of Britain and Germany after World War II present an extraordinary contrast. Two West European democracies, comparatively similar in area and resources, and in the size and educational qualities of their populations, pursued sharply contrasting types of economic policy, derived from sharply contrasting economic theories (though one of the two countries started with far more war damage and vast frontier adjustments, while the other, in due course, discovered extensive oil resources). Moreover, the results (or what followed) over three decades or so could hardly have been less ambiguous according to almost all the usual major economic indicators. (Of course, success according to the usual economic indicators may well be challenged as the ultimate test of policy, and market economies—having previously been condemned for more sluggish growth than those 'purposively' planned under central direction, when they *have* obviously and irrefutably delivered the goods, as in

Germany—are then charged with materialism and 'consumerism'.) Anyhow, for the purposes of comparing the success or failure of two such contrasting policies one could hardly, in the real world, get nearer to the conditions of a controlled experiment—though obviously and inevitably still a long way off.

The question to be asked here is how and why such extremely contrasting types of policy came to be adopted in Britain and Germany after the war, and why, in terms of economic policy, each country took the direction it did, shrinking away from the kinds of policy adopted by the other? How was it that no IEA, if one had come into existence a decade or two earlier, could have hoped for much success in Britain, at the end of the war, with the country dominated so strongly by 'Keynesian' policies and objectives, and even by some vague forms of post-war 'planning'? How was it, on the other hand, that, in defiance of the economic ideas dominant in the victorious countries, Germany was ready for thorough-going market policies, and even uniquely, in nearly a century of Western history, to overturn 'Wagner's Law' and push back the rôle of government in the German economy far beyond what it had been before the war?

THE WRONG LESSONS IN BRITAIN

The answers lie in the contrasting politico-economic histories and experiences of Britain and Germany in the decades since the First World War. Unfortunately for the British electorate and governments in the second half of the 20th century, they learnt the wrong lessons and formed the wrong expectations ('rationally' or otherwise) in developing a fear of deflation, unemployment, and instability, when in the event, for the decades after World War II, the serious dangers were of an opposite kind. On the other hand, the Germans ultimately derived, from a monstrously expensive politico-economic education through experience, what were to be very healthy lessons for the decades ahead: a phobia about inflation, and a sharp awareness of both the inefficiencies and the ugly political dangers of central planning.

Germany also had suffered an extremely sharp, but comparatively brief, deflation (1930-32), which had had the most appalling political consequences in bringing Hitler to power. Moreover, thereafter very high unemployment had been rapidly reduced by 'Keynesian' public spending policies. But, by the end of World War II, these experiences had been completely erased and forgotten in the course of the prolonged sufferings from suppressed inflation, while economic planning was associated with defeat and disgrace. Finally, waiting in the wings, were the men with a masterly version of market doctrines well attuned to the German situation.

Nor was it surprising that the British public, fearing, above all, a return to the 'thirties, granted the central planning and paternalistic social policies of the war years a considerable measure of approval. They were held to have played their part in winning the war and in answering to ideas of 'fairness'. As Mr Paul Addison has observed in *The Road to 1945*,[20] what was later described as the 'Butskellite' consensus had emerged in what he calls 'the revolution of 1940'. Of course Keynesian doctrines should never have been allowed to

[20] Cape, 1975; Quartet Books, 1977.

claim the generality and the dogmatic dominance over policy that they exercised. (No body of economic doctrine should *ever* be granted, as the English classical and, more briefly, the Keynesian doctrines were in Britain, such pretensions to generality and such exclusive dogmatic prestige in real-world policy.) Yet in the 1940s, with the British electorate and parties set on fighting so vigorously the previous peace, no IEA could have been expected to do for Britain what Eucken and Müller-Armack were doing for Germany. 'Outward circumstances', in this country, could, as Mill put it, hardly have been less ready to 'conspire'—which is just what they were doing for the intellectual founders of the *Soziale Marktwirtschaft* in Germany.

VIII. CONCLUSION

Hardly anyone seems to have foreseen the extraordinarily long period of stability and success which the economies of the West enjoyed after World War II. Both the Marxian sympathisers (like Professor Joan Robinson) and libertarian anti-Keynesians (like Professor Hayek) have admitted to a certain surprise. Britain shared in the prosperity which, however, helped for a time to conceal the country's serious underlying problems, as well as the transformation of other problems.

By the early 1950s, with the appearance of regular GNP figures for the leading countries, the relatively low rate of growth of the British economy was being re-discovered. However, the disappearance of the great, overriding inter-war problem of unemployment was a profound relief, and it had given economists of a

Keynesian persuasion—as most of them were—a tremendous boost of confidence in their ability to remove Britain's difficulties. Starting from the fashion for devising countless fantasy growth models, it was proposed that Britain's slow-growth problem could be solved by some combination of 'purposive' planning and a high pressure of demand: monetary policy was to be jettisoned, and stability in the value of money was to be protected by 'incomes policy' or otherwise abandoned as an objective of policy: devaluations would deal with balance-of-payments problems.

KEYNESIAN DEMAND MANAGEMENT AND POLITICAL ENTREPRENEURS

There was much in these fashionable formulae to appeal to political entrepreneurs. Politically, it seemed all too easy. Growthmanship was very much the product of academic economists; but it was the answer to politicians' prayers. Meanwhile, both parties, in the early and middle 1950s, had been beginning to lose their way. By the time the Attlee Government had completed its programme in 1950 the Labour Party was in fundamental disagreement about its ultimate, or even its proximate, objectives. The kind of poverty problems—absolute and relative—in response to which it had come into existence, were now transformed; while, regarding ultimate objectives, the British Labour Party re-asserted Clause 4, at the same time that the German Social Democrats were fundamentally revising their programme and philosophy in the light of the success of the *Soziale Marktwirtschaft*.

On the Conservative side, the promising 'Butler experiment' petered out without the fundamental problems which were looming up being faced, or even discerned. But the elections of 1955 and 1959 were being won by the new governmental weapon of timely Keynesian demand-management. In domestic economics a kind of optimistic, opportunist drift took over, comparable in some ways with the reluctance in the 1930s to face up to the menace of the European dictators. The Thorneycroft resignation of 1958 over public expenditure could be compared with that of Eden 20 years earlier.

The problems looming up in the late 1950s and early 1960s all posed long-term threats to freedom. Creeping inflation was liable at almost any moment to turn into a gallop. The longer-term creep of 'Wagner's Law', with an ever-mounting proportion of government expenditure, approached a possible critical level, at which any halt—let alone a rolling back—would be fiercely challenged, as bureaucratic vested interests were consolidated and fortified by a heightening of trade union powers. Accompanying this complex of threats was a further quickening of Britain's relative economic decline.

'OUTWARD CIRCUMSTANCES' AND THE IEA

By the middle and late 1950s, this was the situation which the discerning (*not* including the present writer) could clearly perceive, and which over the next two decades was to become appallingly more obvious to all but the blindest. And this was where the IEA came in.

In Mill's phrase, 'outward circumstances' were now 'conspiring'. Mill also observed that

> 'the most favourable outward circumstances may pass by, or remain inoperative, for want of ideas suitable to meet

> the conjuncture. But when the right circumstances and the right ideas meet, the effect is seldom slow in manifesting itself.'[21]

Allowing for the immensity and deep-rootedness of the century-long trends in ideas and policy in this country and the power of the vested interests that have become established, it can truly be maintained that, with the IEA's 'right ideas' having met up with 'the right circumstances', the effect has not been slow in manifesting itself.[22]

However, if such long and powerful secular trends are to be turned round, 'the right ideas', even when combined with 'the right circumstances', must, to represent

[21] 'The Claims of Labour', *Edinburgh Review,* April 1845, p. 503; also T. W. Hutchison, 'Walter Eucken and the German Social-Market Economy', in *The Politics and Philosophy of Economics,* Blackwell, Oxford, 1981.

[22] Contrasting, if not contradictory, explanations seem to have been at work in some IEA thinking about the power of ideas. Keynes's famous closing paragraph on the superior power of ideas and the comparative unimportance of 'interests' is inscribed on its walls. But IEA writings also attach much importance to the kind of political analysis (as developed, for example, by the Virginia School) according to which *there is strictly no room for the influence of ideas*. 'Interests', as perceived with certainty by omniscient maximisers, will dominate completely.

Much, or most, of such analysis, like much, or most, of traditional price analysis, is based on a postulate of full knowledge with no uncertainty, implying that individuals know fully and clearly what their interests are and how they are to be attained. Omniscient maximisers under conditions of certainty must be more or less impervious to ideas or persuasion. It is only insofar as the assumption of full knowledge involves an over-simplification, that is, because real people are ignorant and uncertain, that they are open to ideas or persuasion on what their interests really are and how they may be attained.

more than a fleeting, fashionable outcry, comprise a major, dual intellectual contribution, which comprises both general arguments, or an underlying politico-economic 'philosophy', and (possibly much more important) detailed proposals which have a due regard to the historical and institutional conditions of the time. That is what the work of the IEA over the past quarter of a century may be seen to have contributed.

Chapter III

THE EMPHASIS ON MARKET ECONOMICS

D. P. O'Brien
Professor of Economics,
University of Durham

The Author

DENIS PATRICK O'BRIEN was born in 1939 and educated at Douai School and University College, London (BSc Econ., London, 1960, PhD, Belfast, 1969). Assistant Lecturer, Queens University, Belfast, 1963-65, Lecturer 1965-69, Reader 1969-72. He has been Professor of Economics at the University of Durham since 1972. His publications include: *Information Agreements, Competition and Efficiency* (with D. Swann) (1969); *J. R. McCulloch, A Study in Classical Economics* (1970); *The Correspondence of Lord Overstone* (3 vols., 1971); (ed.) *J. R. McCulloch's Treatise on Taxation* (1975); (jointly) *Competition in British Industry* (1974); *The Classical Economists* (1975); *Competition Policy, Profitability and Growth* (1979); *Pioneers of Modern Economics in Britain* (forthcoming). He has contributed to the *Manchester School, Economica, Journal of Industrial Economics,* etc. For the IEA he contributed 'Creating the Optimum Institutional Framework', in *Catch '76 . . .?* (Occasional Paper 47, 1976).

The Emphasis on Market Economics

SYNOPSIS

Academic unease with the market-place stems from a variety of causes including a hostility towards those who operate within it, a preoccupation with technicalities which obscure the realities of markets, and a carelessness about any possible danger to personal freedom arising from interference with entry into and operation within markets.

IEA writings face squarely all three sources of this uneasiness, including the second, for the emphasis is upon content rather than technique.

The areas of interest included by the IEA *Hobart Papers* and other publications have, despite some esoteric examples, covered the mainstream of applied micro-economics.

Contributors have shown intense awareness of the range and subtlety of market forces within a framework of law and custom, especially the generation and diffusion of knowledge, and they have given a special rôle to the entrepreneur who has virtually disappeared from mainstream academic micro-economic literature.[1] Moreover, they have shown that the myth that Oskar Lange

[1] [This 'disappearance' was emphasised by Professor Israel Kirzner and 'confessed' by Professor David Henderson in *Prime Mover of Progress*, IEA Readings 23, 1980.—ED]

and other economists somehow 'solved' allocation under central planning is indeed a myth.

Given the diversity of the IEA contributions, it is impossible, of course, not to have reservations on certain aspects. This contributor is concerned, in particular, that possibilities of market failure are perhaps too readily swept aside, that the hopes entertained for 'internalisation' of externalities through private legal processes are sometimes a little optimistic, that there is a certain ambiguity over income distribution in some of the IEA discussions, and that the possibility of price having a de-stabilising rôle is more or less totally ignored.

These qualifications do not, however, as too many of us have for too long believed, invalidate the fundamental perception of the power, and potential for good, of market forces.

THE EMPHASIS ON MARKET ECONOMICS

1. Academic Opinion and Micro-economic Policy

Academic economists, whose job it is to understand markets, often feel uncomfortable about the operation of market forces. As a distinguished economist, Professor George Stigler of Chicago, of whom the preceding generalisation is not true, has put it:

> 'The intellectual has never felt kindly toward the market place: to him it has always been a place of vulgar men and of base motives. Whether this intellectual was an ancient Greek philosopher, who viewed economic life as an unpleasant necessity which should never be allowed

to become obtrusive or dominant, or whether this intellectual is a modern man who focusses his scorn on gadgets and Madison Avenue, the basic similarity of view has been pronounced.'[2]

SNOBBERY, CONCERN FOR TECHNICALITY, AND CARELESSNESS

There are three sets of reasons for this unease. First, there is a set of attitudes which has been absorbed largely unconsciously during undergraduate education and professional life. These include a snobbery towards 'trade' which, dressed up as a Leftist attitude, has helped to strengthen the anti-vocational bias of British universities under the influence of Oxbridge.[3] Linked with this has been an attitude of disdain, or hostility, towards the entrepreneur and a hostility to advertising which has, at times, bordered on farce.[4] The readiness of people with the best education to assume that they are the only discerning consumers is coupled with a belief in the power of advertising to corrupt which apparently places it far in advance of that possessed by pornography. 'The City' has been firmly fixed in the intellectual mind, at least since Keynes, as something for which contempt—at the very least—is the most suitable attitude.

Such a denigratory attitude does not, however, extend to those employed in capitalist processes; indeed there

[2] G. J. Stigler, *The Intellectual and the Market Place,* IEA Occasional Paper 1, 1963, p. 3.

[3] G. C. Allen, *The British Disease*, Hobart Paper 67, 1976 (2nd Edn., 1979).

[4] [An early IEA project confronted this attitude: *Advertising in a Free Society*, 1959.—ED.]

is what seems at times to amount almost to a conspiracy of silence amongst academic economists about restrictive labour practices. It has been left to the IEA to show, in two distinguished *Papers* from the pens of Peter Jay and Professor J. E. Meade, that concern over these things is not confined to cave-men.[5]

Second, there is a concern with technicalities of economic analysis which not only obscures some tremendously important aspects of the market but makes market solutions apparently remote from reality. This particular aspect of the problem was nicely captured by Professor Stigler, himself no mean technician, who suggested that an economics text written today might begin:

> 'This unavoidably lengthy treatise is devoted to an examination of an economy in which the second derivatives of the utility function possess a finite number of discontinuities. To keep the problem manageable, I assume that each individual consumes only two goods and dies after one Robertsonian week. Only elementary mathematical tools such as topology will be employed, incessantly.'[6]

Third, there is a comfortable carelessness, on the part of those whose employment gives them an unparalleled degree of personal freedom, about any lurking danger to personal liberty. In particular there is the very high risk to personal liberty involved in recent tax legislation enforcement powers, and the dangers posed until

[5] P. Jay, *Employment, Inflation and Politics*, Occasional Paper 46, 1976; J. E. Meade, *Wages and Prices in a Mixed Economy*, Occasional Paper 35, 1971.

[6] Stigler, *op. cit.*, p. 11.

recently by exchange controls.[7] The IEA deserves credit for emphasising these risks, as it does for emphasising also the coercion involved in decision through the electoral process, where the degree of coercion (not only of minorities but also of substantial majorities on particular issues) when matters are decided through a five-yearly ballot on a whole package of issues lumped together in a manifesto, may be considerable.[8]

Even where economic writers agree on general propositions concerning allocation—and at a high level of generality it is quite surprising to find the extent of agreement between economists (the Stalinist relics excepted) on such general propositions—there is still a considerable gap between the propositions and their application to particular situations.[9] Indeed academic writers seem to have great difficulty in applying them at all, except in the most *jejune*, and sometimes idiosyncratically paradoxical, way to particular situations. Although it is true to say that

> 'economists would usually concede that experimentation, enterprise, saving and other economically commendable practices are inhibited by strongly authoritarian political systems',[10]

[7] C. Davies, 'Can High Taxation be Enforced?', in *Tax Avoision,* IEA Readings 22, 1979, pp. 68-72; R. Miller and J. B. Wood, *Exchange Control for Ever?,* IEA Research Monograph 33, 1979.

[8] *The Coming Confrontation: Will the Open Society Survive to 1989?,* IEA Hobart Paperback 12, 1978; *Over-ruled on Welfare,* IEA Hobart Paperback 13, 1979.

[9] Particularly valuable in helping to understand this gap is Samuel Brittan's very perceptive essay, *Government and the Market Economy,* IEA Hobart Paperback 2, 1971.

[10] D. Rimmer, *Macromancy: The Ideology of Development Economics,* Hobart Paper 55, IEA, 1973, p. 59.

it remains true that they frequently adopt positions which involve recommending substantial increases in the economic powers of government. It is undoubtedly true that many—probably the majority—of academic economists were believers, in a purely mystical, even romantic, way in the power of 'indicative economic planning' in the early 1960s. Whether this is some inheritance from the intellectual Left of the 1930s, as has been suggested,[11] I am not sure; but there is undoubtedly much truth in the observation of Professor T. W. Hutchison that 'the phrase "physical controls" still seems to afford an almost sensual pleasure in some quarters'.[12]

2. The Contribution of the IEA to Understanding the Market

(i) *Methodology*

The methodology in IEA Papers is not uniform. In general the IEA is very pragmatic about methodology; although it publishes work by Milton Friedman, very few of the Papers use his methodology. Rather, the methodology is a blend of what, in an excellent recent book on methodology,[13] are called the *analytical* and

[11] 'The leaders who initiated the new phase of British planning . . . and their advisers . . . have been people whose ideas were formed in the intellectual climate of the Western countries in the 1930s when Russia stood out as the model of progressive social and economic thought and the true facts about the cruelties and inefficiencies of her economic system were not yet widely known.' ('Spartacus' (George Polanyi), *Growth Through Competition*, Hobart Paper 35, IEA, 1969, pp. 63-4.)

[12] T. W. Hutchison, *Half a Century of Hobarts*, Hobart 'Special', IEA, 1970, p. 28.

[13] I. M. T. Stewart, *Reasoning and Method in Economics,* McGraw Hill, London, 1979, Ch. 6.

the *moderate-empiricist* positions. The characteristic of the analytical position is that it involves reasoning from common sense and generally acceptable premises about the real world of economic life to deduce what the implications may be of those premises which are not immediately obvious. The characteristic of the moderate-empiricist position is that there is considerable emphasis upon 'validation' or the confrontation of theory with the real-world counterparts of its constructs. The 'analytical' element in the IEA publications is perhaps best represented by much of the material on the nature of the competitive process and, indeed, on the nature of bureaucracy; the 'moderate empiricist' material is best represented by the case studies of particular industrial situations such as transport. The marriage between these two approaches has never been spelt out formally by the principals of the IEA; but it is in part reflected in a statement by Arthur Seldon in a Preface:

> ' "Theory" does not denote a realm of thought remote from the real world; it is rather a reinforcement of insight by observation designed to explain the real world.'[14]

Such an approach, by its emphasis upon contact with the real world, moves at a much simpler technical level than is now common in economic writing. Interestingly enough, the result is to increase the degree of illumination, particularly in matters of public finance.[15]

[14] *Prime Mover of Progress: The Entrepreneur in Capitalism and Socialism,* IEA Readings 23, p. xi.

[15] See in particular *Taxation: A Radical Approach,* IEA Readings 4, 1970, and *The State of Taxation*, IEA Readings 16, 1977, especially Professor I. F. Pearce's comments on optimal tax theory, pp. 110-111.

TESTING AGAINST THE REAL WORLD

It is a mark of the method of reasoning employed in the IEA publications that the propositions do permit of some comparison with experience. Because of the 'analytical' element in the IEA writings, the reader instinctively tests premises against casual empiricism; and because of the 'moderate-empiricist' elements the IEA Papers themselves exhibit a considerable emphasis upon factual studies. This has been particularly marked in the *Eaton Paper* series with its discussions of matters such as trading stamps, corporation tax, errors in man-power forecasting, disclosure in company accounts, and details of wage rates and labour markets. It is clear that the Institute attaches importance to accurate and detailed micro-economic data. This is a particularly valuable part of its work: for economists are often prepared to assent to broad propositions about the power of market forces while accepting the word of non-economists that the circumstances of a *particular* market situation make a market solution either impossible or unsatisfactory. This, in itself, is not necessarily a bad thing; a little humility on the part of economists is always welcome. But it often serves as an excuse for (i) neglect of detailed factual studies—which have, in any event, little academic standing—and (ii) adopting a suitably 'progressive' (i.e. corporatist) attitude towards situations in which market forces can be extremely efficient allocators and in which 'market failure' is likely to be of small degree compared with 'government failure'.

The Institute itself, through its principals Ralph Harris and Arthur Seldon, is to be applauded for its use of questionnaires to try to establish preferences on welfare, even though such survey work,[16] like that which attempts to establish the positions of demand curves, suffers from the fact that the preferences might be different if people really had to experience a pain in the wallet. Such a consideration certainly justifies a degree of caution in interpreting the survey results; but it does not justify dismissing them out of hand because they do not happen to accord with the critics' political prejudices.

Given the ultimately inconclusive nature of most economic argument, the end-result of all this endeavour may, of course, simply be to increase the range of logical possibilities which may be considered in a particular policy situation such as deficiency of finance in local government.[17] But that itself can be extremely valuable. As linear thinking (the emphasis on long chains of reasoning from very limited premises) has increasingly replaced lateral thinking (the ability to draw together a wide variety of disparate elements to form a composite picture) in economics, the tendency to limit the range of possibilities to be considered in any particular problem has become increasingly marked.

(ii) *The areas of interest*

The range of IEA Papers, covering virtually all topics in applied economics, is remarkable. Attention should not be distracted by some of the more esoteric examples

[16] R. Harris and A. Seldon, *Over-Ruled on Welfare*, IEA Hobart Paperback 13, 1979.

[17] Particularly interesting in this respect are some of the possibilities canvassed in I. Papps, *Government and Enterprise*, Hobart Paper 61, IEA, 1975, and in R. Harris and A. Seldon, *Pricing or Taxing?*, Hobart Paper 71, IEA, 1976.

—blood, animal semen, and entrepreneurship in sport —from the very solid range of achievement in dealing with mainstream topics. For the vast majority of IEA publications covers industrial structure and competition (with particular emphasis upon restrictive practices), externalities, agriculture and food, fuel, transport, international trade and payments, financial institutions, the labour market, public (i.e. government) income and expenditure, inflation and growth, economic development, housing and land, the social services and inequality, and education. Particularly interesting have been such studies as those by Dr Christina Fulop of the rôle of private employment agencies, demonstrating the benefit of a competing private sector,[18] and of the marketing of central heating which showed the critical importance of advertising in the working of a competitive economy,[19] the detailed investigations of restrictive practices on *both* sides of industry,[20] and Professor Alan Walters's study of transport.[21]

This last drew four lessons from the study of transport which have much wider applicability. They were, first, the identification of the fallacy of pressure for an 'inte-

[18] C. Fulop, *Markets for Employment,* IEA Research Monograph 26, 1971.

[19] C. Fulop and R. Harris, *Marketing for Central Heating,* IEA Research Monograph 4, 1966.

[20] F. Knox and J. Hennessy, *Restrictive Practices in the Building Industry,* IEA Research Monograph 1, 1966; D. S. Lees, *Economic Consequences of the Professions,* IEA Research Monograph 2, 1966; G. Hutton and J. Hennessy, *Source-Book on Restrictive Practices in Britain,* IEA Research Monograph 7, 1966.

[21] A. A. Walters, *Integration in Freight Transport,* IEA Research Monograph 15, 1968.

grated' transport system based upon the belief that government has superior knowledge of the needs of transport users, and that it is worthwhile sacrificing all the present advantages of flexibility for a cost advantage which may, in any case, not materialise. Second, that the cost of centralised knowledge—which is far higher than the cost of decentralised knowledge—can be too high. Third, that the knowledge problem is only part of the difficulty—there is also an implied assumption that the knowledge obtained by government will be used by it in a disinterested way. Finally, that licensing constitutes a barrier both to entry and to flexibility in resource use. Also very valuable was the study of effective protection,[22] the early emphasis on the effects of housing policy on the labour market,[23] the impressive and well-documented study of bread by Dr Duncan Reekie, the predictions of which were neatly borne out by events,[24] the attack upon the International Air Transport Association (IATA) monopoly which argued persuasively that this simply led to excess capacity not increased safety,[25] and the very important *Hobart Paper* by Dr Wilfred Beckerman advocating charges on pollution.[26]

[22] S. J. Wells, *The Shape of Britain's Tariff*, IEA Research Monograph 17, 1968.

[23] H. Gray, *The Cost of Council Housing*, IEA Research Monograph 18, 1968; also Norman Macrae, *To Let?*, Hobart Paper 2, IEA, 1960.

[24] W. D. Reekie, *Give Us This Day . . .*, Hobart Paper 79, IEA, 1978.

[25] M. H. Cooper and A. K. Maynard, *The Price of Air Travel*, Hobart Paper 53, IEA, 1971.

[26] W. Beckerman, *Pricing for Pollution*, Hobart Paper 66, IEA, 1975.

THE ECONOMICS OF POLITICS

Undoubtedly the most significant single area of interest which the IEA has explored has been that of the economics of politics. This starts from the recognition in an editorial Preface of 'the simple-minded hope, still common in some circles, that public expenditure is good because it is public',[27] but broadens out into a study in several Papers, by Professors Gordon Tullock, Charles Rowley, W. A. Niskanen and others, of the workings of both bureaucracy and of elected government. It is particularly enlightening because of the presumptions which pervade most of the mainstream literature on the rôle of government in economic life—the imposed social-welfare function and the myth of the omniscient and impartial government, analysed by Professor J. M. Buchanan.[28]

The declared aim of the *Hobart Paperbacks*, to study 'the influences which affect the translation of economic ideas into practical policy and the nature of economic activity in public affairs',[29] is clearly in accord with the interest in the economics of politics. But it also leads to the position that the public readiness to have selective welfare benefits is a matter to be investigated,[30] not accepted on trust from the assertions of politicians, a position which is particularly important when minor-

[27] Preface to I. R. Hoos, *Systems Analysis in Social Policy,* IEA Research Monograph 19, 1969, p. 4.

[28] *The Economics of Politics,* IEA Readings 18, 1978, especially the contribution by C. K. Rowley, pp. 24-29; and G. Tullock, *The Vote Motive,* Hobart Paperback 9, IEA, 1976.

[29] E.g. Preface to S. Brittan, *Government and Market Economy, op. cit.,* p. vii.

[30] A Seldon, *Taxation and Welfare,* IEA Research Monograph 14, 1967.

ities of up to 49 per cent can have their preferences overruled by 51 per cent—or by a smaller minority—under the British electoral system.

(iii) *The perceptions*

It is no exaggeration to say that the contributors to the IEA Papers manifest an awareness of the range and subtlety of market forces which escapes the textbooks. We start from the valuable reminder of a truth which was well known to Adam Smith but which has simply escaped the consciousness of many modern economists—that competition is a highly artificial institution requiring the rule of law.[31] Within this framework price, as Hayek has emphasised, summarises a great deal of information, much of it not otherwise quantifiable. Prices operate through the market not only to supply information but also for the purposes of allocation, decision, incentives, and co-ordination.[32] Competition has a vital rôle to play not only in diffusing existing knowledge but also, as the 'Austrian' Professor Israel Kirzner explained,[33] in the generation of new knowledge.

The IEA's contributors have done a great deal to explore the real nature of competition. The blinkered view of the nature of competition common in economic

[31] O. Gélinier, *The Enterprise Ethic,* IEA, 1968.

[32] See also S. Brittan, *Participation without Politics*, Hobart Paper 62, IEA, 1975, p. 53, which draws on A. Lindbeck's outstanding *The Political Economy of the New Left* (1971). An important discussion of the significance of unquantifiable and possibly unidentifiable variables which may yet be summarised in price is in I. R. Hoos, *Systems Analysis in Social Policy,* IEA Research Monograph 19, 1969.

[33] 'The Primacy of Entrepreneurial Discovery', in *Prime Mover of Progress, op. cit.*

literature is one of the penalties which have had to be paid for the mathematisation of economics. General equilibrium and Pareto optimality, which are the stock-in-trade of the technically-trained economist, certainly lack the fundamental knowledge-creation and diffusion characteristic of real competition; indeed, there is not any very clear way that they could incorporate it. Yet this characteristic is by far the most important of decentralised competition. The many-faceted nature of true competition makes appraisal of a competitive situation by the criteria of 'perfect competition' particularly unhelpful. As Professor S. C. Littlechild has emphasised, competition must be seen as a dynamic process of discovery and co-ordination taking place over time, rather than in a static sense.[34]

This rôle of the market in discovery and co-ordination helps to focus doubt on the rôle of government as the corrector of market failure. Government *cannot* have knowledge of much of the relevant information necessary to correct market failure, because it is highly subjective. Indeed, Littlechild has argued persuasively that all the data in marginal-cost-pricing models are not given, and it is the task of the manager to find out what they are, to discover what products consumers want, what resources and techniques are available, and what prices are likely to be paid. In securing the fulfilment of such tasks, by large numbers of individuals, the market has great advantages over command systems which sacrifice personal liberty and suffer from inadequate

[34] The outstanding IEA discussion of the nature of competition is in S. C. Littlechild, *The Fallacy of the Mixed Economy*, Hobart Paper 80, 1978. See also C. Fulop, *Consumers in the Market*, IEA Research Monograph 13, 1967.

feedback of information as well as failing to provide adequate incentives to the individual.[35] All this, as Samuel Brittan has pointed out, indicates that the idea that allocation under a command system was somehow 'solved' by Oskar Lange, and that computers could in some way replace the market, is a myth.[36] It is the *responsiveness* of the economic system, not the extent of departures or otherwise from statically optimal prices, which is the key welfare question.[37] Change is necessary in all economies, and historical experience indicates that it is less, not more, harsh in competitive economies than in totalitarian ones.[38] In the last resort, the market system works: and it does not depend on prison camps and special shops for the privileged élite to make it do so.

IMPORTANCE OF ENTREPRENEURIAL ALERTNESS

In all this the entrepreneur has a very special rôle,[39] one which was recognised by Alfred Marshall, but which has receded into the dim background since we started, in Friedman's phrase, to 'walk with Walras'. Entrepreneurial profit plays a vital rôle in stimulating alertness to new opportunities, while the competitive framework in which the entrepreneur has to operate provides the essential managerial discipline.[40] Particular markets

[35] S. Brittan, *Participation without Politics, op. cit.*, p. 15.

[36] *Ibid.*, p. 54.

[37] *Ibid.*, pp. 70-1.

[38] Gélinier, *op. cit.*, pp. 109-113.

[39] Littlechild, *op. cit.*; Gélinier, *op. cit.*; *Prime Mover of Progress, op. cit.*, especially the contribution by Kirzner, pp. 7, 18-19.

[40] Gélinier, *op. cit.* p. 18.

which arouse the suspicions of academic economists, such as forward commodity and financial markets, are important even where they yield positive rents to some of the participants.[41] The speculation which yields such rents can have a stabilising and socially useful rôle to perform. Markets and market forms are not static; and the spontaneous market creation of the Euro-dollar system is one example of the way in which the search for knowledge can produce beneficial evolution which is able to absorb forces with which the previous market form would have had difficulty in coping.

In the dynamic concept of the market, advertising has an important rôle to play by stimulating search, by widening the range of possible consumption patterns available to the consumer (and thus increasing the possibility of realisation of economies of scale and new technology), and also, perhaps ironically, by helping to inoculate consumers against the danger of being too easily persuaded.[42] The IEA contributors have not only stressed the value of the market; George Polanyi and others have also pointed out that there is no criterion for government action which can effectively replace the market.[43] There is no rational basis for the allocation of resources and the adoption of targets by planners and they therefore, both in the USSR and the free world,

[41] Cf. the contribution by A. A. Walters in *Government and the Land*, IEA Readings 13, 1974; and *City Lights: Essays on Financial Institutions and Markets in the City of London*, IEA Readings 19, 1979.

[42] Cf. e.g., C. Fulop, *Consumers in the Market, op. cit.*, and, in particular, G. C. Allen, *Economic Fact and Fantasy*, Occasional Paper 14, IEA, 1967 (2nd Edition 1969).

[43] E.g. G. Polanyi, *Planning in Britain: the Experience of the 1960s*, IEA Research Monograph 11, 1967, and others.

take the industry forecast and turn it into a target which has to be met. Even if this expedient is successful, which it almost never is, it removes the vital element of flexibility and adaptability which is *the* great virtue of the market system.

Outside totalitarian systems much 'planning', of course, has been based upon a naïve macro-economic approach; and it is much to the credit of the IEA that its contributors emphasised the importance of having micro foundations for macro-economic policy rather earlier than became fashionable amongst the majority of professional academics.[44] But even where Western economies have not been explicitly planned, there has been substantial government allocation of resources; and the IEA contributors have emphasised the point, not always well appreciated, that administrative solutions can have very high resource costs,[45] although not always perhaps emphasising sufficiently that the major problem with such solutions is that they lack the market's adaptive ability and so become overtaken by circumstances. But they have pointed out the sub-optimality involved in zero pricing, the opportunity cost of wasteful public procurement in terms of schools and hospitals foregone,[46] and, as Alfred Marshall foresaw long ago, the replacement of the cost-minimiser by the grant-maximiser in markets where government plays

[44] G. Polanyi, *Short-Term Forecasting: A Case Study*, 1973; also L. M. Lachmann, *Macro-economic Thinking and the Market Economy*, Hobart Paper 56, IEA, 1973.

[45] E.g. R. McKie, *Housing and the Whitehall Bulldozer*, Hobart Paper 52, IEA, 1971.

[46] E.g. K. Hartley, *A Market for Aircraft*, Hobart Paper 57, IEA, 1974.

a substantial active rôle.[47] They have emphasised, too, as John Stuart Mill perceived,[48] that a state monopoly of supply can pose real threats to the individual[49] and that, in evaluating public supply, real-world markets, with all their faults, have to be compared with real-world politicians, civil servants, and 'experts'.[50]

Perhaps most interesting in dealing with these same faults of real-world markets has been the emphasis by

[47] *Ibid.*, p. 67.

[48] 'One thing must be strenuously insisted on; that the government must claim no monopoly for its education, either in the lower or in the higher branches; must exert neither authority nor influence to induce the people to resort to its teachers in preference to others, and must confer no peculiar advantages on those who have been instructed by them. Though the government teachers will probably be superior to the average of private instructors, they will not embody all the knowledge and sagacity to be found in all instructors taken together, and it is desirable to leave open as many roads as possible to the desired end. It is not endurable that a government should, either *de jure* or *de facto*, have a complete control over the education of the people. To possess such a control, and actually exert it, is to be despotic. A government which can mould the opinions and sentiments of the people from their youth upwards, can do with them whatever it pleases. Though a government, therefore, may, and in many cases ought to, establish schools and colleges, it must neither compel nor bribe any person to come to them; nor ought the power of individuals to set up rival establishments to depend in any degree upon its authorization. It would be justified in requiring from all the people that they shall possess instruction in certain things, but not in prescribing to them how or from whom they shall obtain it.' (J. S. Mill, *Principles of Political Economy*, ed. W. J. Ashley, Longmans, 1923, p. 956.)

[49] S. Brittan, *Participation without Politics, op. cit.*, pp. 33-5; see also *ibid.*, p. 92, on Friedman's point that victims of McCarthy-ite persecution found refuge in the private sector; J. S. Mill, *Principles of Political Economy, op. cit.*, p. 956.

[50] Brittan, *op. cit.*, p. 37.

IEA contributors such as Beckerman upon the desirability of internalising externalities[51] (as well as recognising that externalities result from the activities of the public as well as of the private sector and occur in communist as well as in free countries).

Such insights into the economic system, and concentration upon the possibility of 'government failure', make it easy for those studying the public sector to explain such matters as the fact that cuts by bureaucrats will be those that hurt most and do least good[52]—there is a public sector ratchet; that one of the powers possessed by planners is that to bestow wealth through their modification of property rights (the late Professor F. G. Pennance);[53] and that there is a critical link between property rights and economic incentives (Chiplin and Coyne).[54]

3. Some Reservations

In defence of the IEA it should be said that it does not hold firmly to a party line and that its contributions are very much less monolithic than I have made them appear by summarising what seem to me some of the most important aspects. There is no attempt to present a complete, internally consistent, party line. One engaging example of this is that the volume on *Tax Avoision* contains some entertaining yet sinister quota-

[51] E.g. Beckerman, *op. cit.*

[52] *The Taming of Government: Micro/macro disciplines on Whitehall and Town Hall,* IEA Readings 21, 1979.

[53] *Government and the Land, op. cit.,* especially the contribution by F. G. Pennance.

[54] B. Chiplin, J. Coyne, and L. Sirc, *Can Workers Manage?,* Hobart Paper 77, IEA, 1977.

tions from a former member of the Mafia about doctors, seeking outlets for earnings on which tax has been evaded, becoming ensnared by 'the Mob';[55] while worries about the possibility of such developments in this country, in the event of the NHS being replaced by private medicine, are not apparent in the discussions of health care.

Nevertheless, taking the IEA's contributions as a whole, there are a number of emphases about which this particular reader is not entirely happy and, if not universal, they are often not confined to one single author. As a matter of history of economic thought, it seems to me that the claims for the analysis of the market to be 'Austrian' are dubious. Though it may be necessary to invoke some slightly questionable academic pedigree in order to re-assert the fundamental nature of the competitive process, a truth of which many economists have all but lost sight, it may equally not be helpful to associate this analysis with a body of ideas which, taken as a complete package, is much less persuasive and attractive than the analysis of the market as a dynamic process of knowledge creation and diffusion.

ANALYTICAL ISSUES

(i) *Possible market failure in health and education*

On a number of analytical issues I think that some reservation about the predominant approach in IEA publications is not unreasonable. In particular, it seems to me that in medical care the possibilities of market failure arising either because of ignorance on the part

[55] *Tax Avoision, op. cit.*, p. 64.

of the consumer or because of moral hazard are often treated too lightly. Moreover, like the 19th-century Turkish Empire, the NHS is continuously represented, not least by Arthur Seldon, as on the verge of collapse. As with the Turkish Empire, one may feel a certain cynicism about this attitude. The discussion of vouchers and loans in education seems to me to have taken advantage of the destruction of the grammar and secondary modern schools and to imply that the present comprehensive system is the best that state education can offer (although I readily concede that the rapid destruction of the old system constitutes a serious warning against a state monopoly of education); and the payment of benefit from the 'right-hand pocket to the left-hand pocket'[56] is not *necessarily* wrong. For if there were conclusive evidence that money left in the right-hand pocket would be spent on betting, not on education for children or health care, which would thus inflict a welfare loss on children and costs on the community, then I for one would vote for transferring money from the right-hand pocket to the left-hand pocket—at least if government could be trusted to do it properly. Since, however, support for such intervention by government is the norm, it is perfectly reasonable for IEA authors to put the other case. In doing so they may help us to question seriously the need to transfer money from one pocket to the other (passing it through a civil servant in the process) and to make sure that protection of the unprotected is really involved in such a process.

[56] A. Christopher, G. Polanyi, A. Seldon, B. Shenfield, *Policy for Poverty*, IEA Research Monograph 20, 1970, p. 89.

(ii) *Internalising externalities*

The zeal of IEA authors to internalise externalities is commendable; and it is valuable to be reminded that external effects are not immoveably external. But the attitude that such effects can frequently be internalised by a re-definition of property rights and reliance upon private legal actions takes a perhaps over-sanguine view of the working of legal processes and rather begs the question by neglecting the need for an improvement in court procedures. It also takes insufficient account of the fact that reliance upon legal remedies discriminates against the poorer, less legally-conscious, sections of the community. Since IEA authors in general object to 'ear-marked redistribution',[57] they would not presumably welcome an extension of the legal aid service to deal with this kind of problem. There are, indeed, obvious objections to such a course.

(iii) *Income distribution*

In this connection it seems to me that there is a certain ambiguity over income distribution in the IEA Papers, and particularly over the income effects of using price. The attitude of IEA economists is that you should take care of income distribution separately, *via* a negative income tax. But in order to be effective as a means of redistribution, such a system might have to use very high marginal rates of tax in order to provide sufficient redistribution. It is open to IEA economists, of course, to answer that rationing by queue also has income effects—because people cannot use their existing

[57] [Except for education and health where market information through experience is lacking (or deficient).—ED.]

income for the purchase of the good or service which is in short supply. Since rationing by queue also distorts allocation and therefore reduces total income, it also has more subtle income effects which may be extremely damaging. But a great deal here depends on relative magnitudes; and the IEA discussions do not always appear to me to be sufficiently sensitive to this point even though it does not affect the validity of the basic perceptions about resource allocation.

Reservations about income effects are perhaps particularly in order in relation to the housing market; and it seems to me that there is some inconsistency between the very understandable concern shown by IEA authors over the state of the housing market in this country and the recognition by Henry Smith that public housing has been very important in the development of Hong Kong.[58]

(iv) *Market failure again*

Just occasionally it seems to me that the possibility of *increased* external effects, in the event of a market solution, is swept aside a little bit too abruptly. I accept that it does not require much intelligence to find fault with market forces but that it requires a far higher degree of skill than governments customarily show to do better (Professor Colin Robinson).[59] But, to take one instance, if private transport were allowed to compete with London Transport it is not inconceivable that some of the evils associated with the 'pirate buses' of

[58] H. Smith, *John Stuart Mill's Other Island*, IEA Research Monograph 6, 1966.

[59] C. Robinson, *The Energy 'Crisis' and British Coal*, Hobart Paper 59, IEA, 1974.

yesteryear might return. One of the IEA's critics, Professor David Collard, has made what seems to me a perfectly fair point about externalities—such as hygiene—arising if rubbish collection were a private service;[60] and there are other areas, such as the use of pesticides and of antibiotics in animal feedstuffs, where attention to the problem of externalities seems warranted.

(v) *Industrial concentration*

In dealing with industrial structure it does seem to me that the IEA's admirable record in combating restrictive practices is somewhat marred by the apparent willingness of some contributors to allow considerable freedom to mergers and the market for corporate control. Indeed, there seems to be some complacency about increasing industrial concentration. Similarly, while I agree that the Monopolies Commission reports on detergents and on Roche Pharmaceuticals (particularly the latter) were too facile, I do not share the apparent unwillingness of many IEA contributors to recognise that market power may be abused even where it does not spring from the existence of restrictive agreements.

(vi) *De-stabilising speculation*

In dealing with the rôle of price it seems to me that the possibility of de-stabilising speculation and, more generally, of positive feedback, is ignored. This seems to me to be true both in dealing with agricultural and

[60] D. Collard, *The New Right: A Critique*, Fabian Tract 387, 1968.

financial institutions. In this connection it might be noted that the 'Cobweb Theorem'[61] is conspicuous by its absence from IEA publications.

(vii) *Problem of bureaucracy*

Finally, it seems to me that the analysis of bureaucracy is not always entirely well-conceived. In particular, the problem with bureaucracy is not primarily that its output is too large; the resources used in bureaucratic input, and the levying of taxes to pay for an output which may actually be quite small, but which uses up a great deal of resources, is surely more important.

CONCLUSION

Such reservations are inevitable when one reads through the quite remarkably large output the Institute has managed to produce. But these reservations do not invalidate the basic perceptions which inform the IEA's contributions; they widen the range of considerations which have to be taken into account but they do not automatically invalidate others. The basic mistake which too many of us have made for too long is to afford so much weight to the qualifications that they come to be regarded as completely neutralising the primary arguments in favour of market pricing.

[61] A shorthand term for a market situation in which, because of lags in the adjustment of supply, negative feedback, which is normally stabilising, may actually move price away from equilibrium.

Chapter IV

AN AMERICAN PERSPECTIVE
From 'Markets Work' to Public Choice

James M. Buchanan and Gordon Tullock
Center for Public Choice, Virginia Polytechnic Institute

The Authors

JAMES MCGILL BUCHANAN has been University Professor of Economics and Director of the Center for Study of Public Choice at the Virginia Polytechnic Institute, Blacksburg, Virginia, since 1969. Previously he was Professor of Economics at Florida State University, 1951-56, University of Virginia (and Director of the Thomas Jefferson Center for Political Economy), 1956-68, and University of California at Los Angeles, 1968-69.

He is the author of numerous works on the economics of politics and public choice, including *The Calculus of Consent* (with Gordon Tullock) (1962) and *The Limits of Liberty: Between Anarchy and Leviathan* (1975), and he has contributed to four IEA Papers, the latest being (with Geoffrey Brennan) *Monopoly in Money and Inflation* (Hobart Paper 88, 1981). Professor Buchanan is a member of the IEA's Advisory Council.

GORDON TULLOCK is University Distinguished Professor of Economics and Public Choice, Virginia Polytechnic Institute and State University. Universities of South Carolina, 1959-62, Virginia, 1962-67, and Rice, 1967-68. Editor of *Public Choice*. Author of numerous works including: *The Politics of Bureaucracy* (1965); *Private Wants, Public Means* (1970); *The Vote Motive* (1976) and contributions to *The Economics of Charity* (IEA Readings 12, 1974) and *The Taming of Government* (IEA Readings 21, 1979).

An American Perspective

I. INTRODUCTION

We have been careful to entitle this paper 'An American Perspective' rather than anything more general. In the initial invitation, we were asked to discuss the Institute as viewed by American 'public choice economists', an invitation that in itself suggested the restrictiveness of our vantage point. While we do hope to discuss the IEA in a somewhat wider context than that of 'public choice', narrowly conceived, we make no claim to represent mainstream or orthodox American attitudes, to reflect 'establishment' opinion, whether reserved for the limited group of applied economists or extended to describe the intelligentsia.

DECISIONS AND INSTITUTIONS

In the first of these settings, that of applied economics (often labelled as 'public policy'), we are perhaps somewhat less sympathetic to the main thrust of the IEA's efforts over the quarter-century than those of our American counterparts who have, in their own researches, paralleled the IEA thrust more closely. In a real sense, 'public choice' research is more 'institutional' than straightforward applied economics. 'Public choice' examines more carefully the political, or government and bureaucratic structures, rules, and procedures (the *institutions*) through which policy decisions are made, and less the *content* of the decisions themselves.

Having said this, however, we should hasten to add, indeed to emphasise, that it is through the IEA's efforts that Public Choice research has been brought to the attention of the academic-intellectual-journalistic community in Great Britain. These efforts were expressed particularly in the IEA's 1978 and 1979 symposia on the 'economics of politics', in which both of us participated,[1] and in the publication of several of our works, along with those of others who represent Public Choice, broadly defined.[2] There is, indeed there must be, a close relationship between constructive research in applied economics (or public policy) and in Public Choice, the 'science' or sub-discipline that examines more directly the means through which policy programmes are chosen and implemented.

THE MARKET WORKS

In six words or less, what has been the thrust of the IEA's research programme? 'The market alternative works'. This has been the central hypothesis of most of the IEA's efforts in positive economic analysis (of what *is*). The demonstration of the validity of this hypothesis, in one industry, occupation or other application after

[1] *The Economics of Politics*, IEA Readings 18, 1978, and *The Taming of Government*, IEA Readings 21, 1979.

[2] Gordon Tullock, *The Vote Motive*, Hobart Paperback 9, 1976; J. M. Buchanan, R. E. Wagner, John Burton, *The Consequences of Mr Keynes*, Hobart Paper 78, 1978; W. A. Niskanen, *Bureaucracy: Servant or Master?*, Hobart Paperback 5, 1973.

another, has, in a more or less natural progression, allowed the normative imperative (of what *should be* done—policy) often to be stated as: 'Try the market', or, even more concisely if with some apologies to the King's English, 'privatise'.[3]

Comparably, the thrust of the research programme in Public Choice may be somewhat sketchily put as: 'The governmental-political alternative does not work'. Research in Public Choice has concentrated on the way government functions. As a result it has been discovered that commonly *the government alternative is inherently inferior to the market.* There have been two positive implications, one of which is to shift much government activity to the market and the other is to change government structure so as to improve its efficiency. The central 'government fails' hypothesis, again in numerous applications in IEA Papers, has been demonstrated in positive analysis of varying degrees of analytical rigour. Again, given the analytical support of the hypothesis, the conclusion for policy often becomes: 'Try the market' or 'Privatise'.

THE CHANGE IN POLICY

The two research themes seem to converge, therefore, at the level of the normative implication of what should be done. There remains a difference, however, and one that deserves some discussion. The imperative, as stated briefly, may be directed differently. The central message may be aimed at the attitudes of political leaders, in party councils or legislative chambers, and at the supporting attitudes of the general public. The im-

[3] [Or, even more colloquially, 'suck it and see'.—ED.]

plementation of the imperative involves a shift in attitudes followed by an explicit *change in policy*.

Council houses, for example, are sold; airlines are de-regulated. By comparison with this more direct approach to desired policy shifts, Public Choice aims its message at the institutional structure through which policy is made and changed. It aims at more comprehensive, and long range, reform as opposed to piecemeal, pragmatic change. Public Choice, in its normative dress, suggests that mere shifts in policy are likely to be temporary, and that effective reform lies only in a modification of the rules that allow legislatures to enact good (or bad) policy. With a well designed legislature the kind of error which involves detailed interference with the ordinary workings of the market should be much less likely than with current structures. Further, constitutional limitations on such intervention may be desirable, although here the possibility that the constitution can always be changed puts limits on what can be done. This structural reform involves much more than the limited claim that enlightened politicians should not enact legislation involving such detailed interference with the working of markets.

II. THE TRANSMISSION OF IDEAS

The whole set of questions concerning the transmission of ideas, particularly those with potential political impact, is highly important. Unfortunately, we know relatively little here. The only reasonably rigorous model for idea transmission through society is a direct transcription of the theory of contagious diseases developed by medical scientists. The resemblance between a contagious disease and the spread of an idea may not be immediately obvious, although perhaps many would regard the analogy as helpful in explaining the spread of Marxism. The similarity, however, is in practice quite strong. In both, a person who has a particular germ or a particular idea contacts someone else and either does or does not transmit the germ or idea. Whether the disease or idea spreads throughout the population depends on the frequency of contact and the ease with which it may be transmitted.

In both contagious diseases and ideas there may be means of transmission other than direct person-to-person contact. A germ or an idea may lie dormant for considerable periods (the idea in a forgotton book in the library) and then be picked up and begin to spread. Further, there exist mechanisms for what you might call mass transmission: a city water supply for disease or the mass media for an idea. Unfortunately the mathematical model of transmission is very hard to use, even in the contagious diseases where it was invented. It would be even more difficult to 'model' the spread of ideas. Mathematically the two processes might perhaps be treated as mappings of each other, but this correspondence may be of little help granted that the mathematics is apparently much too difficult for practical application in either case.

In human society ideas not only have to be spread; they also have to be invented. In this respect there is a difference between Public Choice and the IEA. The Institute has mainly devoted itself to spreading ideas that were in existence. Public Choice, on the other hand, has been more concerned with inventing new ideas, or, at the least, the discovery of new applications for established methods of analysis. We should not over-simplify here, and we do not want to stress the contrast. The IEA has, of course, been responsible for the development of original ideas, and Public Choice has included considerable effort to spreading ideas already in existence. Nonetheless, and by its own acknowledgment, the Institute to a large extent has devoted itself to the propagation of ideas that have been in existence for quite a long time, but which had been largely forgotten. The development of new ideas, particularly new applications of neo-classical economics, has increasingly become an important aspect of the Institute's work, but, over the quarter-century, this has remained considerably less important than the spreading of old, valid but neglected ideas.

III. PUBLIC CHOICE AND THE IEA: TEMPORAL COHORTS

The Institute is what it says it is. An institute that is physically located in London, with influence that extends over Great Britain and many other countries. It may seem folly to attempt any comparison of an 'Institute' with what can be best called a 'sub-discipline', *Public Choice*, which as such is not located at any place,[4] and which is described best as a method of research. Such a comparison is not quite the apples and oranges that it may seem, however, when we recognise

[4] Although we like to think that our own Center for Study of Public Choice at Virginia Polytechnic Institute does offer a locational focus for the more inclusive effort.

that the IEA and Public Choice are temporal cohorts. Both have emerged full grown in the quarter-century spanned by the mid-1950s and the early 1980s. The research emphasis, both of the Institute and of Public Choice, reflects a reaction against that of mainstream economics over the period. Keynesian macro-economics was still in its phase of delusionary grandeur in the middle 1950s,[5] when both were founded.

NEGLECT OF MICRO-ECONOMICS

In late 1980, it is hard to remember the situation at the time the IEA was founded. Even in the United States, where the situation was not so extreme as in Britain, micro-economics had been substantially replaced by macro-economics as the active field for applied economic policy. The situation was perhaps unique in history. Most economists had, of course, studied micro-economics and courses in it continued to be taught. Indeed, early editions of Samuelson's textbook, *Economics*, devoted about half of their pages to micro-economics. And articles on micro-economic problems continued to be published in the economic literature.

Nevertheless, in a real sense, micro-economics was largely forgotten. The existing frontier was macro-economics. Government policy advisers in the USA and Britain hardly ever turned their attention from macro-economic questions. (In the United States, a partial exception was present in the work of economists in the Rand Foundation who commenced work in defence

[5] 'Economic policy in immediate postwar decades was dominated by the writings of John Maynard Keynes. An almost idolatrous adoration surrounded him.' (Lord Balogh, 'Is Keynes Dead?', *New Republic*, 7 June 1980, pp. 15-18.)

economics.) Samuelson's textbook, although half micro-economics, presented the macro-economics first, and presumably many teachers of elementary economics never got around to the 'tedious' chapters on micro-economics.

All of this has, of course, changed since the 1960s. In part the change came simply because the macro-economic models do not seem to fit the present-day world. In part it came because economic advisers began to get nervous about offering any kind of macro advice. (On one recent occasion in a meeting of the American Economic Association, Gordon Tullock asked Robert Solow what advice could be given to President Carter. Solow, a leading Keynesian macro-economist replied, 'I sympathise with your question'.)

Micro-economics probably remained largely unknown to many of the post-1950s economists who were trained in the post-war years. They may have been compelled to take micro-economics courses, but both they and their instructors thought of this analysis as some rather tedious bit of the history of the discipline, more or less like Latin. Even for those who learned the lessons, there was little or no interest in applications. The whole policy literature was dominated by Keynesians, or by economists whose political positions suggested that Keynesian methods and tools were more appropriate to their purposes.

BREAKDOWN OF COMMUNICATIONS

There were, of course, many scholars, both economists and scholars in other fields, who still remembered the older ideas. But communication among them had broken down. They tended to be isolated individuals in clusters of one or two at particular universities and there was very little interaction among them, in part because the orthodoxy was so much dominated by the opposing policy thrust. Those who sensed that there was something wrong with the then-prevailing macro-economic orthodoxy, but who themselves did not have a background in classical economics at all, were even more unfortunate. They tended to be critics who did not themselves have anything in the way of a coherent position of their own. These critics of the existing system felt cut off and isolated, and willing to turn to almost any expedient. But they were not capable of developing a coherent counter-position simply because of the breakdown in communication.

The situation in Britain was in many ways worse than in the United States, and when Antony Fisher founded and Ralph Harris and Arthur Seldon developed the Institute of Economic Affairs, they may well have thought of themselves as voices crying in the wilderness. However, they had much to build on. The halcyon days of classical political economy had not been wholly forgotten, and there were many individuals who were still interested in the neo-classical economics of Marshall. A first step was to put these scholars in better communication with one another by providing a format for publication, which would at the same time have the effect of transmitting the ideas to a wider audience. The Institute could and did both stimulate research and development of a coherent point of view by permitting the existing scholars with a pro-market approach to communicate with one another and at the same time provide for their ideas to be more widely disseminated.

THE ESCAPIST MATHEMATICAL PRIESTHOOD

By contrast with the origins of the IEA, Public Choice did not emerge specifically as a reaction against a macro-policy emphasis. Its origins were based on a somewhat more general reaction against the pervasive neglect by economists (and political scientists) of the political-governmental *institutions* through which any policy, micro or macro, must be implemented. Both the IEA and Public Choice have served as counterweights to the proclivity of modern economists to engage themselves predominantly in escapist mathematical rigour, spurred by some apparent effort to create a priesthood defined by an ability to communicate one with another in a language inaccessible to all non-members.

The counterweight objectives have been successful to a degree; the apogee of formalism[6] in economic theory has been reached, and its most skilful practitioners now turn their minds to the sobering reality of the world as it exists. In this respect, the IEA, perhaps largely due to the editorial persuasiveness of Arthur Seldon, has been more successful than Public Choice. In the latter, the mathematical properties of some of the complex collective choice problems have proved too tempting to the prospective priests, and there has been no Arthur Seldon to ride herd over a rapidly growing sub-discipline.

[6] [Formalism in macro-economics was analysed by Professor L. M. Lachmann in *Macro-economic Thinking and the Market Economy*, Hobart Paper 56, IEA, 1973.—ED.]

IV. IDEAS, EDUCATION, AND LITERATURE

The IEA's very successful rôle in the transmission of 'market works' ideas took two forms. The first and most conspicuous is, of course, the very well worked out dissemination activity carried on by the Institute. No-one who has ever had lunch at Eaton Square or Lord North Street can fail to be impressed with the Institute's ability to penetrate the 'establishment' of Britain. But the success of 1981 in these respects is built on hard work in days when the IEA was not so conspicuous as it now appears. Indispensable for the successful public relations activity was the development of a body of literature which countered the then-dominant conventional wisdom.

A student in Oxford who might have been assigned a paper on some government policy would have found some difficulty in obtaining economic analysis outside the prevailing Keynesian-benevolent despot orthodoxy before the IEA's list. All of this changed with the Institute's steady and respected series of publications, first from Hobart Place, then Eaton Square, then Lord North Street. With time, over the quarter-century, the development of a battery of publications by the IEA covering substantially all policy matters provided a firm intellectual basis for opposition to the collectivist orthodoxy. Further, this set of publications provided an indispensable base for the more direct educational activities. These, of course, have far more immediate impact on policy. In the long run, however, the publication series may have had even more impact through its influence on the younger generation of scholars and then through them eventually on the public.

It should not be forgotten, however, that the efforts in education and publicity have a somewhat similar long-range effect. An individual politician, civil servant, or even journalist, who is introduced to an unorthodox point of view is likely to continue for a very long period to remain aware of the existence of such unorthodox points of view and willing to pay attention to them. He may indeed be converted, with the result that there is a long-range effect there too. Further, the educational activity no doubt had a good deal to do with the fact that the scholarly publications attracted a fairly wide readership. As authors of several IEA Papers we should like to feel that the widespread press attention they got simply reflected their merit. But we cannot fail to notice that when we publish under other auspices, and especially in the United States, we do not get nearly so much general public attention.

As we noted in II, the process of spreading ideas through society is not well understood. It is not possible to say for certain that the quite significant change in economic attitudes in Britain over the quarter-century is the result of IEA activities. We can say for certain that it is not solely the result of the Institute. Nonetheless, the Institute has found what appears to be a sensible and successful strategy. It involves a well-organised combination of scholarly publications and public dissemination which has proved successful, made so in part by the skill and devotion of the people in the IEA, but also in part because of the special nature of British society over the quarter-century.

If, however, the intellectual climate in Britain is radically different in 1981 from the one that existed when the IEA was founded, this does not imply that the IEA has won a war. What we really should say is that the first skirmishes have gone very well. The major battle is not yet won, but it would seem sensible to continue with the same general strategy.

V. WHY NO AMERICAN IEA?

It has long been common among American friends of the IEA to ask ourselves why no comparable institution exists in the United States. Some attempt to answer such a question can perhaps indicate something of our own American perspective.

At the outset, we shall state categorically that we are pleased that the IEA does not, and cannot, have an American equivalent. We state this while at the same time we should emphasise that, were we British citizens, we should indeed value highly the net contribution of the IEA. Most simply put, the United States has no IEA because it has no London. Despite its claims to emergence as the national cultural centre, and despite the horrendous growth of the bureaucracy, Washington, even in the early 1980s, remains a closer relative to Canberra or Brasilia than it does to London. We should have to imagine New York, Boston, Washington, Chicago, New Orleans, Los Angeles, San Francisco rolled into one to create some United States analogue to London.

Why is this geographical dispersal relevant in examining the potential for an American equivalent of the IEA? The IEA has remained at the centre of the British establishment, whether intellectually, culturally, commercially, or politically defined, but, at the same time, it has not been 'captured' by the establishment. This somewhat peculiar, but highly productive, stance would not have been possible in Washington, even with the devotion, wisdom, and integrity of Ralph Harris and Arthur Seldon. Transplanted onto the District of Columbia turf, the IEA would have, we venture to suggest, become at least partially captured by the pressure-backed political-legislative-bureaucracy jungle, and hence largely incapable of exhibiting the long-range coherence of purpose that has been its London hallmark.

VI. CONSTITUTIONAL REFORM, PUBLIC CHOICE, AND THE IEA IN 2006

When the IEA commenced operation in 1957, its argument to the effect that 'the market alternative works' was not directly in the mainstream of current economic policy discussion in Britain. In the setting of that time, this argument was indeed 'way out', a facet of history that is difficult even for us who lived through it to recall. The quarter-century has been characterised by a catching-up, by a dwindling distance between the concerns of the IEA and the concerns of those 'experts' who offer advice and counsel on economic affairs of the day, on *current policy*. As we indicated above, the war of ideas has by no means been won on the ways in which economic policy is shaped and directed. And surely the IEA's challenges in these more or less traditional areas of emphasis remain large.

CONSTITUTIONAL REFORM: A LEAP FORWARD

At the same time, however, the IEA should make efforts to 'leap forward', to establish or re-establish some considerable distance between some of its research focus and that of the economic policy politics of the 1980s. And, to those of us who work in *constitutional* analysis and design, the IEA's expressed interests in Public Choice in 1978 and 1979 are highly encouraging. This shift of emphasis suggests to us that, over the next quarter-century, the events of politics may later be described as a 'catching up' with ideas of those 'academic scribblers'[7] who now talk about basic constitutional change, about reform in the structure of political order.

As with the 'markets work' argument of the mid-1950s, the 'constitutional reform' argument of the 1980s will be, and will be seen to be, somewhat remote from the expressed concerns of current policy advocates. But Public Choice, in its positive aspects, has taught us that policy programmes emerge from and are directly influenced by the structure of the institutions through which decisions are made.

Teaching the lessons of elementary micro-economics, elementary price theory, to separate generations of elected or potentially elected public leaders will, of course, remain a noble cause. But it will remain folly to rely on the ignorance and illiteracy of past and present politicians as the only source of hope for a better record of achievement over the second quarter-century of the IEA's history. Political leaders, along with those who support them, deserve to be examined and analysed as everyone else, with enough insight to understand their individual interests, broadly defined. But if this minimal step is taken towards re-interpreta-

[7] [J. M. Keynes, *The General Theory*: the passage from which this phrase originates is quoted in full by A. J. Culyer in Chapter V, p. 115.—ED.]

tion, attention is necessarily drawn to the structure of the institutions, and to the incentives, the rewards and penalties, for the persons who act within the constraints of such institutions. Do the potential leaders really need the lessons of elementary economics so much as to be allowed to act within a reformed structure of institutions?

Unfortunately, perhaps, there is no ready-made discipline to draw on in constitutional analysis that is remotely comparable to that of classical and neo-classical political economy. The 'markets work' argument was an application of an established discipline, even if sometimes forgotten in the Keynesian delusion. But things are different when we come to discuss constitutional reform. Orthodox political science or government, as an academic discipline, offers little here. But the wisdom of the 18th century can be re-evaluated, and it can come to inform the minds of modern men. The 18th-century scepticism about the abilities of politics, of government, to handle detailed regulatory tasks, to go beyond the limits of the 'minimal' or 'protection' state, is an attitude of mind that is capable of attainment.

A RADICAL CHALLENGE TO THE IEA

What specific steps might be taken by the IEA in the early 1980s that would ensure progress in the direction indicated, over and beyond the acknowledged interest in and promotion of understanding and application of Public Choice? The importance and relevance of political and legal philosophy must be recognised. Comparative research on alternative constitutional and governmental structures can been encouraged. The work of economists and other scholars who have managed to remove 'majoritarian parliamentary democracy' from the realm of the sacrosanct can be published.

In sum, it is time for the IEA, in part at least, to become *radical*, in the literal meaning of this term, to seek out and explore the ultimate sources of social order. The 'markets work' ideas promulgated by the IEA from 1957 were radical in the intellectual setting of the Britain of that time. These ideas have now become topical currency. Our plea is for the IEA to invest some of its resources in making a new leap forward, to shift dramatically beyond the boundaries directly relevant to policy, to encourage and sponsor research and discussion of constitutional structures that may seem fixed in concrete to orthodox mentalities. So conceived, the challenge for the second quarter-century can be equally important and equally exciting as that for the first.

Chapter V

THE IEA'S UNORTHODOXY

A. J. Culyer
Deputy Director,
Institute of Social and Economic Research,
University of York

The Author

PROFESSOR A. J. CULYER is Deputy Director of the Institute of Social and Economic Research at the University of York. He has taught at several universities here and abroad and been a visiting professor at Queen's University, Kingston (Canada) and the University of Otago (New Zealand). He has held senior visiting research posts at the Ontario Economic Council and the Australian National University.

His books include *The Political Economy of Social Policy* (1980), *Economic Aspects of Health Services* (1978), *Measuring Health—Lessons for Ontario* (1976), *Need and the National Health Service* (1976), *The Economics of Social Policy* (1973) and *Health Economics* (1973). He has published some 80 articles, pamphlets and monographs.

He is married with two children and is organist and choirmaster in a rural Yorkshire parish church, which local monopoly of opportunity for the performance of his amateur musical compositions is alas denied him in economics!

The IEA's Unorthodoxy

Like so many other things in life, being an IEA author has a private and a public aspect. While the latter is of most interest to readers of a volume such as this, the opportunity Arthur Seldon's kind invitation to contribute this piece affords me to mention the former is too attractive to pass over and enables me also to discharge a debt of honour.

PRIVATE ASPECTS

I begin therefore with the reflection that the major private advantage I have had as an IEA author is the opportunity to have got to know the IEA's moving spirits. The advantage is not merely that of counting amongst one's friends subtle intellectual entrepreneurs who have, despite assertions one occasionally hears to the contrary (and also probably despite temptations to do the contrary), insisted on diversity in politics and ideology in selecting and 'bringing on' their authors. The unity in this diversity comes of course from the central commitment to neo-classical economics and to its use wheresoever its logic seems applicable.

The great and private advantage I have in mind is not this, however, but lies simply in the benefit I, and I am sure innumerable others, have derived from the Institute's editorial skills in preparing a manuscript for publication. If I know my faults in penmanship, as I think I do, it is largely due to the IEA's editorial promptings. My besetting sins are teutonic, being excessively given to polysyllabic portmanteaux and long sentences with large numbers of subordinate clauses vying for primacy in the race to get a tangle of ideas out. In a word: pomposity. (At one's worst one can be both pompous *and* elliptical!) As any editor knows, the will of an author to sharpen his prose is inversely related to his need to sharpen it. One of Arthur Seldon's great gifts has been the ability with grace and tact to accomplish just that. Needless to say, my sins still beset me —though I hope I have improved a bit. But they beset me least when my manuscripts have had the IEA pencil across them.

The earliest piece I wrote for the IEA was a tendentious Paper on blood[1] with Professor Michael Cooper. Unfortunately I no longer have the drafts on file, nor the accompanying correspondence, and so I am not able to analyse the stylistic impact of the IEA on my own final draft. Out of curiosity, however, I have made a statistical comparison of another piece of writing published at the same time, which was also non-technical in nature (but which I prefer not to identify!). The average sentence length in this piece was 33·5 words, compared with 28·8 in the piece for the IEA. The average word length was 5·0 letters compared with 4·6. This is for an arbitrary selection of passages of roughly equal length. The standard deviation[2] of sentence length

[1] *The Price of Blood,* Hobart Paper 41, IEA, 1968.

[2] The standard deviation is a measure of the variability of data. For a symmetrical bell-shaped distribution of sentence lengths

[*continued opposite*]

in this other piece was 14·9 words and 13·9 in the IEA piece. The standard deviation of word length was 2·6 letters in each. This is effective corroboration of part at least of what it means to be edited by the IEA, and I have cause to be grateful for it.

ACADEMIC LABELLING

To become an IEA author is to become publicly labelled. The most conspicuous label is political: one is wrongly identified as a member of a philosophical tradition (libertarianism), a supporter of a political party (Conservative), a part of a trendy political fad (the 'New Right'), or a follower of an eponymous school (a 'Friedmaniac'). I suppose to be labelled with all four tags is to be labelled a 'Thatcherite'.

It takes only a couple of conspicuous IEA authors in an economics department for it likewise to become labelled. I have often been asked by people who really know my politics what it is like to be at York, whose economics department has often been associated in both the public and the professional mind with the IEA political label. Professor Maurice Peston, in an otherwise generous brief review of my *The Economics of Social Policy*,[3] wrote:

> 'The book itself is reasonably dispassionate; in particular, managing to avoid the worst excesses of the debate for

having a mean of 28·8 words, about 68% of all sentences lie between one standard deviation below and above the mean, viz. between 14·9 and 42·7 words. For the other article, 68% of sentences were between 18·6 and 48·4 words long.

[3] Martin Robertson, London, 1973. This book now has a new incarnation as *The Political Economy of Social Policy*, Martin Robertson, 1980.

and against market solutions to social problems. Considering its origin at York University, this is a triumph in itself.'

At the time I think five economists at York had published with the IEA—out of a total of about 55 full-time academic economists then actively researching and writing in their subject. The political views represented in the department seemed to me rather characteristic of most British economics departments with most corresponding roughly to the liberal socialist Crosland position in the Labour Party and a range varying from 'moderate libertarian'[4] on the 'Right' to non-Marxist socialist on the 'Left'. The distribution of opinion among senior staff was not markedly different from that among junior staff.[5]

I am tempted to suppose that labelling as grotesquely non-descriptive as this is merely mischievous. Yet I suspect it betrays a profound necessity among not only the politically aware public but also in academic economic coteries for a short-hand means of sorting one's reading material. A political label for economists interested in policy is a handy way of identifying 'friends' and 'enemies', of locating literature that will or will not shock or upset, of alerting one to the necessity (or not) of having particular critical wits about one —for knowing authors' political views alerts one to

[4] The qualifying adjective is there as I have yet to find a York economist not in favour of substantial wealth redistribution, especially inherited wealth.

[5] Today, the York department is even less to the right than hitherto. When Michael Jones-Lee, that most humane and kindly of men, departed for a chair at Newcastle, the joke went around that both economics departments had thereby moved to the left.

possible analytical 'blind spots'. If so, dependence on political labels is a measure of economics' immaturity as a discipline: an immaturity we prefer to deny but which, if it exists, requires a means by which one may come to terms with it.

I do not think that such labelling has any really serious dangers inherent in it (so long as we avoid paranoia). The main one, if it is indeed a danger at all, arises from the inefficiency of the label as a description of the thinking it is supposed to describe. That is evidently true when it comes to labelling economics departments. It is also true when it comes to labelling individuals. None of the political labels mentioned above describes at all accurately my own politics. But then I know from my own experience that the inefficiency of the labels is well-known: sufficiently well-known for my own work (whether for the IEA or others) not to be read only by, or only sympathetically by, those whom these labels *would* describe and sufficiently well-known for many whom these labels most definitely do *not* describe to seek appointments in the York economics department.

IEA POLITICS

Too much, however, should not be made of this public political labelling: one can be paranoid in one's search for a conspiracy of the 'Right'—a sign that the idea is being taken too seriously. Nonetheless, there *is* a distinctive 'political' quality about the IEA and we *all* know it. I think it resides in four interrelated characteristics:

- an overt editorial emphasis on micro-economics;
- an overt editorial emphasis on *applied* micro-econ-

omics—that is, the application of explicit economic analysis to a specific problem;

- an overt editorial emphasis on the *economic* side of public policy questions to the (deliberate) neglect of other issues relating, for example, to social justice;
- the dearth of easily identifiable socialist economists among authors.[6]

It is the fourth of these features that gives the political labels their plausibility and the three preceding ones that largely give rise to the fourth. There is no strict *logical* necessity here, but there are powerful connections that lie within what one may call the sociology of economics. For one thing, the Left (particularly the Marxist Left) has not been much interested in micro-economics since the last war. For another, nearly all the post-war pioneering analyses by economists of *social* policy have come from the Right: externality analysis, human capital theory, property rights theory, subsidy theory, 'funny money' (vouchers and all that), the theory of the family, filtering[7] in housing, theories of racial and other types of discrimination. The rather uniform concern of economists who can in broad terms be thought of as 'left of centre' with macro-economic analysis on the one hand and micro-economic description on the other is bound to be reflected in the authorship of the IEA's Papers given the micro-economic intent of the

[6] Arther Seldon, who knows these things better than I, estimates that 20 per cent of his authors would describe themselves as having sympathies left of centre.

[7] 'Filtering' refers to the process by which housing is allowed to depreciate, split into sub-units, etc. such that the owner's return on his asset is maintained even in the presence of rent controls, changes in demand, etc.

IEA and its enterprising aim to get the analysis applied wherever the logic seems applicable.

INADEQUATE EMPHASIS ON INCOME REDISTRIBUTION

The great exception has been in the economics of income redistribution. This has not been much represented in the IEA's lists outside a set of publications dealing specifically with negative income taxation and some on poverty.[8] But the whole subject of income redistribution has seen quite major advances in the post-war period, many of which (I think *most* of which) have come from economists like Atkinson, Lerner, and Sen who are broadly speaking of the Left. I must say that this seems to me to have been an inconsistency in the IEA's editorial policy, for the analytical underpinning of most of this analysis has been the familiar micro-economic analysis of the neo-classical school and its utilitarian close relation in political philosophy and ethics.

It is particularly striking that the three principal contenders for theoretical primacy in the modern philosophical analysis of distributive justice are deeply imbued with economic reasoning: modern utilitarianism shares, of course, the same 19th-century heritage as modern economics in its concern for welfare; Rawls's theory of justice as 'fairness' is remarkably Paretian in its central contractarian concepts;[9] Nozick's theory of

[8] *Policy for Poverty*, Research Monograph 20, 1970; Colin Clark, *Poverty before Politics*, Hobart Paper 73, 1977.

[9] The idea of a social contract is common in political philosophy. In Rawls's work it refers to a conceptual experiment akin to 'putting yourself in someone else's shoes'. The proposition is that, under such experimental conditions, each will reach the same conclusions about what is 'fair'—a kind of social contract.

the just or minimal state is heavily influenced by economic theories of property rights. Since distributive justice is a study in which socialist economists have always been active, a more active editorial policy here would most likely have brought about a higher proportion of socialist IEA authors. Moreover, since the majority of economists have always evinced great interest in this subject, and still do, the IEA would have performed a useful educational rôle in popularising the debates that have taken place and in making the sophisticated analysis that underlies them more accessible to students and the lay public.

HEGEMONY OF THE 'RIGHT'

I cannot think of a very satisfactory reason why there should have been—as I believe there has—such a hegemony of the Right in the development of key ideas for the analysis of social problems (setting aside redistributive matters). It is tempting to attribute it, at least in part, to a failure of the Left seriously to come to terms with the instruments of social policy as distinct from its ends. In my own socialist days I know I was impatient with those who tempered their enthusiasm—or who sought to temper mine—with behavioural questions that cast doubt upon the efficacy of the means that being a socialist committed one to. It did not seem necessary to ask *why* the behaviour of management in publicly-owned industry should differ from that of management in the private sector: you removed the profit motive and gave them rules to work by, derived from a theoretical description of what ought to be. It did not seem necessary to ask *how* the National Health

Service allocated its resources, or *how* utilisation patterns by patients might change: leaving decisions to the technical experts (mostly medical) and removing the so-called price 'barrier' was enough to get 'needs' properly met. You did not really ask *why* harmful external effects arose from capitalist activity nor why they should not in a socialist society.

It came as an extraordinary revelation to me to discover that so many men of the Right actively cared as much about the ends of policy, and from an essentially similar humanitarian-cum-individualistic view that I had always thought the monopoly of my friends of the Left. (The idea that they have a monopoly of virtue was and is one of the less endearing features of socialists.) It was even more disconcerting to find that the Right pushed their individualism a good deal further—in particular asking questions about how individuals would act under differing constraining environments, whether they are individuals authorised to make decisions on behalf of others in their capacity as politicians, representatives, managers and so on, or individuals simply making decisions on their own behalf in their capacity as house owners, consumers, patients and so on.

LIBERTARIAN ECONOMICS AND ENGLISH SOCIALISM

The point of this autobiographical detour is not, of course, to record the shattering impact of an American libertarian graduate economics school upon the liberal socialist graduate of a provincial English university. Rather, it is to suggest that the behaviourist questioning of modern neo-classical economics as found in IEA

Papers is bound to be sceptical of the classic socialist remedies, for socialism was not, and is not, only concerned with ends but also with means. But if the means can be challenged—even accepting the decent and liberal ends about which I found there was less disagreement than I had thought (which is not to say there was no disagreement at all)—then socialism too was being challenged. Since I too believed at the time that socialists had a monopoly of decency, the temptation to dissociate oneself from this powerful threat was enormous.

I like to think, of course, that I resisted the temptation. The difficulty was that it left one without a handy label to describe one's politics—one's friends might think one had deserted the noble cause. Worse still, there was the danger of having one (or all) of the tags applied to oneself that I have asserted tend to get attached to IEA authors. In any event, I conjecture that this commitment of the Left not only to a particular view of decency and social justice but also to a specific means of bringing them about has been largely the reason why it has been left to the tougher-minded libertarian Right to develop the theoretical innovations I have mentioned. This has been something of a tragedy, partly because the social ends sought by socialists are not of course the same as those of the libertarian Right (though, as I have said, many are shared), and hence the tools developed may not be developed in ways appropriate to tackle the problems thought important by socialists, and partly also because intellectual initiatives have passed increasingly to the Right and it is new ideas that capture the imagination—particularly of young intellectuals. Few will deny, I think, that the agenda of political debate in recent times has increasingly been set by the Right at every level of public discussion. It is also scarcely surprising that the IEA has been an important part of this rising tide, both reflecting it and forming a part of its generation.

Even more fundamentally, it would be a tragedy (I say 'would be' not 'is' because the tragedy has not—quite—happened yet) were it to come about that these theoretical tools be seen as useful instruments only for analysing problems of little concern to the Left, or as tools not capable of being usefully wielded to further any of the ends (possibly even the means) of the Left. My own fervent belief is that they are there for us *all* to use and although, as I suggest later, political partiality can serve a useful purpose both in the advancement of knowledge and in the improvement of the lot of man, were partiality ever to become divisive in this way—in further bolstering and perpetuating mutually hostile and non-communicating schools of economic thought—both these noble causes would suffer incalculable harm. There may be irreconcilable differences between economists, but they do not have to be carried further than logic requires. Not to use tools of analysis on the simple ground that the opposition invented them is not required by logic. It is symptomatic of paranoia. (I should add that the Left does not have a monopoly of paranoia either.)

ECONOMIC IMPERIALISM

Another aspect of the public labelling that attaches to IEA authors relates to the topics selected for application of micro analysis. IEA policy has been extraordinarily adventurous in encouraging the application of economic analysis in unwonted places.

Most definitions of economics are notable for describing a method of tackling a general and unspecified set of problems arising out of scarcity. Until the 1950s, what economists *did* in practice was almost invariably to tackle *financial* questions: concerning the production and allocation of money-priced goods and services. This entirely conventional restriction of the *technique* to a particular set of *topics* was completely shattered by the IEA's policy, which rapidly earned it (and its authors) a reputation for tackling the 'uneconomic', for going 'beyond' economics, and for 'economic imperialism', as topics again conventionally treated by other disciplines like sociology and political science were seen as no less amenable to economic analysis than those in its conventional territory.

This revealing distinction between *topics* and *modes of analysis* has been extraordinarily fruitful and has generated some very lively and instructive debates. Social philosophers, political scientists and sociologists have increasingly absorbed economic ideas into the corpus of their own thought. A university subject like social administration (which is not a discipline at all but is instead characterised by the *topics* studied and its *multi*-disciplinary perspective) has become transfused with economic thinking as a complement to the other disciplines used to study its topics. As a result it has become incomparably stronger, more relevant to policy questions, and worthy of serious intellectual respect.

Consider the diversity of topics treated in the IEA's publications:

– traditional topics of economics such as business organisation and finance, international trade, money and credit, public finance and taxation;

- a whole range of social policy questions including health, education, pensions, and poverty;
- newer kinds of institutional economics concerning the economic analysis of *government* (as distinct from the analysis of government economic *policy*) and bureaucracy (in both public and private organisations);
- a whole range of specific 'firsts' including the economic analysis of blood, garbage, deck chairs, animal semen, cricket, marriage, and a whole range of restrictive practices in the building industry, financial intermediaries, the legal, medical and other professions, and elsewhere.

In addition there have been occasional ventures into political philosophy, particularly emphasising the political economy of various concepts of liberalism.

To have accomplished all this, and to have accomplished it in language that is comprehensible to the general reader, is an achievement in which any IEA author may be proud to have shared. May the next 25 years be as productive, stimulating—and irritating—as the last!

THE MARKET FOR THE IEA'S WORK

Most IEA publications consciously address themselves in the Preface to a particular readership. Thus:

> 'The purpose . . . is to contribute a stream of authoritative, independent and lucid analysis to the discussion of economic policy in industry and government'

or

> 'it is hoped they will be of special value to students and

teachers of economics as well as to laymen interested to know what economists are thinking and writing on government and industry'.

We see here two characteristics of all IEA Papers: relevance to policy and popularisation of economic ideas by 'professionals'. I use 'professionals' as a shorthand for 'practising economists' though I must confess I dislike its connotations: economists are not 'professionals' in the sense that they act as agents for their clients (save in consultancy), nor are they 'professionals' in the sense that they control entry and terms of service of their 'members'. Nonetheless it is characteristic of the IEA that it has mostly commissioned 'professionals' to do the popularising, rather than some other group of interpreters of economic thinking. It is I think notable that the exceptions—Papers written by or addresses given by others, such as men of affairs, politicians—are among the least successful of the IEA's publications.

I ought to qualify that judgement since my own perspective is that of the academic economist. Accordingly, I tend to judge success or failure in terms of the usefulness of IEA Papers as teaching aids and as sources of summary information about topics and issues remote from my own major interests. It may, therefore, be that non-'professional' writing for the IEA has an impact (for example, on policy-makers) of which I am unaware.

I detect, however, that my own criteria for success are probably those the IEA itself would choose. Editorial policy, for example, has quite explicitly encouraged authors not to feel constrained by what they may regard as 'politically possible'. One reason for this may be that the authors are poor judges (many doubtless are) of the 'politically possible'. More generally, however, it seems to me that the IEA has taken the long rather than the short view of policy-relevance. Its hallmark is the thinking through of a policy issue in specific publications and, by a cumulation, the exposition of a general mode of thinking applicable to a wide range of policy issues. It is therefore scarcely surprising that one of Keynes's most famous dicta is often found in IEA editorial utterances (I quote at fuller length than is customary):

> '. . . if the ideas are correct . . . it would be a mistake, I predict, to dispute their potency over a period of time. At the present moment people are unusually expectant of a more fundamental diagnosis; more particularly ready to receive it; eager to try it out, if it should be even plausible. But apart from this contemporary mood, the ideas of economists and political philosophers, both when they are right and when they are wrong, are more powerful than is commonly understood. Indeed the world is ruled by little else. Practical men, who believe themselves to be quite exempt from any intellectual influences, are usually the slaves of some defunct economist. Madmen in authority, who hear voices in the air, are distilling their frenzy from some academic scribbler of a few years back. I am sure that the power of vested interests is vastly exaggerated compared with the gradual encroachment of ideas. Not, indeed, immediately, but after a certain interval; for in the field of economic and political philosophy there are not many who are influenced by new theories after they are twenty-five or thirty years of age, so that the ideas which civil servants and politicians and even agitators apply to current events are not likely to be the newest. But, soon or late, it is ideas, not vested interests, which are dangerous for good or evil.'[10]

[10] J. M. Keynes, *The General Theory of Employment, Interest and Money,* Macmillan, 1936, pp. 383-4.

I cannot resist supplementing this with my favourite quotation from an even greater economist (Marshall):

> 'Enthusiasm for the idea in faith, in hope, and in charity is the best of human possessions; and the world owes very much to those who have been thrown off their balance by it. But, on the other hand, a responsible student of social problems must accept mankind as he finds them; and must base his estimates on that which is practicable. He must nourish the idea in his heart; but his actions, his conversation, and even his thought must be occupied mainly with the actual: he must resist every temptation to make a short cut to the ideal. For indeed a traveller in a difficult country, who makes for his ultimate goal by a straight course, is likely to waste his time and strength and perhaps to meet disaster.'[11]

While I doubt whether any IEA editorial room has either of these quotations prominently displayed, they might as well be there on the walls. Taking the long view, and tempering reformist zeal not by current perceptions of what is practicable but by what is known of the nature of man and the niggardliness of Nature, is one of the strengths of the IEA. For teaching purposes I have always found those IEA publications with a clear theoretical focus to have been the most useful. The hardest thing students have to learn is how to apply theory to practical problems. Hence the special *forte* of the IEA in analysing specific problems has made it an important contributor of teaching material: its importance lying less in the substantive issue analysed than in demonstrating how a practical problem can be tackled

[11] A. C. Pigou, 'In memoriam: Alfred Marshall' in A. C. Pigou (ed.), *Memorials of Alfred Marshall*, Kelley and Millwan, 1956, pp. 83-4.

using usually only elementary theoretical propositions.

I would rate this contribution as more fundamental and more useful than its rôle in stimulating reconsideration of conventional attitudes—at least for teaching purposes. But there can also be little doubt that the IEA has had an important substantive rôle in the way economists and men of affairs think about both specific policy questions and policy questions in general. Contemporary British policy debates about, for example, resale price maintenance, vouchers and loans for education, reverse income taxation are unthinkable without the IEA's Papers. At the more general level, those of its publications that have adopted a clearly individualistic line in political philosophy have, quite independently of their substantive specific content, contributed a valuable stream of articulate thinking about economic affairs in general and one without which, again, much current debate would be unthinkable.

Thus, although IEA authors have in some cases probably had a short-term impact on contemporary policy issues, the IEA's markets lie less among people with day-to-day policy-making responsibilities than among those who help to frame the context in which policy-making will take place, that is, among those who teach and are taught and those whose opinions 'count' —the politically aware intelligentsia.

SOME MERITS OF PARTIALITY

Although I feel the IEA would be yet stronger and achieve its educational ends more effectively had its authors been more representative of the whole spectrum of political positions held by users of the neo-classical paradigm, yet one may argue that the IEA's impact on contemporary economic thinking might as a consequence have been less. I remember once upsetting Professor Gordon Tullock (at a lunch at the IEA) with the proposition that knowledge would be more effectively advanced in a world of scholarship in which scholars were less committed *personally* to what they wrote: that debate and the discovery of new ideas were best promoted by the adoption of positions that one may not wholly 'believe in' or even believe at all. What is important is that, since the market in ideas more closely approximates the model of pure competition than many other markets, truth—if we may so grace our scholarly objective—is best seen as the outcome of this competitive interaction rather than as something we must aspire to as individuals. Thus, take an argument and develop it to, or even beyond, the limits of what one believes reasonable. Take an argument, and play devil's advocate as hard as one can. Take an argument, and care not what motives or beliefs are ascribed to you in taking it. To feel a scholarly moral obligation only to publish what one believes to be right is appropriate scholarly ethics where scholars are monopolists but unnecessary (and harmful to the scholarly cause we support) under competition in a world of specialists where the 'generalist' has become almost extinct.

Gordon Tullock was uncomfortable, of course, because he believes what he writes, and does not write what he does not believe. Perhaps such a commitment is a necessary psychological condition for intellectual innovation (Tullock is of course a fruitful innovator). Perhaps this psychological need operates also with institutions (like the IEA) as with individuals. Perhaps it is necessary for an institution like the IEA to have a distinctive label that associates it with a particular set of commitments in order that it may effectively market its wares—that survival in the market for ideas, especially the popularising market, depends upon a distinctive commitment and this accounts for the success of institutions like the Fabian Society and the IEA.

Be all that as it may, I feel confident that few will disagree that the IEA's contribution over the last 25 years has had a *creative* impact not only upon people in sympathy with those holding the distinctive political position I mentioned earlier. If this is true, and if the IEA has had as strong an impact upon people out of sympathy with its own versions of the liberal tradition as it has on those who see themselves within it, then my point is made: partiality pays. Moreover we can *all*, regardless of political affiliation, join enthusiastically in the birthday greetings that, in my judgement as both author and reader, the IEA so richly deserves.

Chapter VI

MARKET FAILURE AND GOVERNMENT FAILURE

David Collard
Professor of Economics,
University of Bath

The Author

DAVID COLLARD has been Professor of Economics at the University of Bath since 1978. He was born in 1937 and educated at Tiverton Grammar School, Devon, and Queens' College, Cambridge. He was formerly Senior Lecturer in Economics at Bristol University and Lecturer at University College, Cardiff. He is author of *The New Right: A Critique*, Fabian Tract 387 (1968); *Prices, Markets and Welfare* (1972); *Altruism and Economy* (1978); (ed.), *Income Distribution: The Limits to Redistribution* (1980). For the IEA he wrote 'Immigration and Discrimination: Some Economic Aspects', in *Economic Issues in Immigration* (IEA Readings 5, 1970).

Market Failure and Government Failure

I. A PERSONAL NOTE

When Arthur Seldon asked me, a long-standing critic of the Institute's work, to write this Chapter I took out my long spoon (now tarnished through lack of use) and recalled first supping with the Devil. In 1968 I wrote a little Fabian Tract, *The New Right: A Critique*, which was critical in tone and (worse) carried an aggressive cover illustration (not of my doing) which was taken to be an offensive caricature of one of the Institute's authors. Ralph Harris and Arthur Seldon responded handsomely by inviting me for a long, friendly and stimulating discussion on social policy over a buffet lunch. They later even invited me to contribute a chapter to a book on immigration.[1]

This initial encounter with the Institute illustrates, I suppose, the courtesy and energy of its two remarkable intellectual entrepreneurs, their genuine interest in ideas and, for me most important, their willingness to truck with the enemy. Recalling that encounter and subsequent meetings I know they would not wish me, in this volume, to play the part of a licensed fool who must please or be cast out. This essay is therefore offered in

[1] *Economic Issues in Immigration*, IEA Readings 5, 1970.

the spirit of friendly criticism of a triumphantly successful institution.[2] I leave others to judge whether its success is due to the superiority of its ideas or simply to a political lurch to the 'Right'. But I cannot fail to note (after 20 years of teaching students) that the ready availability of up-to-date and well-written analytical policy papers must have made an impression on generations of students.

I find it convenient to start with my earlier criticisms of the Institute. My *Tract* was written rather quickly in the Spring of 1968 because I was aware both of the growing influence and quality of its work and of a tendency among academics and others to discuss it as 'cranky' and right-wing. In writing it I read pretty well everything the Institute had produced: I have not been able to carry out as detailed a search for the later period! I expressed my fears at the time as follows:

> 'My worry is that the left is being successfully outflanked by the New Right. While we argue about possible (marginal) extensions of public ownership, the really important hard core of the public sector (health, education and other social services) is being undermined. We are now at the beginning of a series of major assaults on the welfare services and rather than foraging around in the public sector we should look to our defences.' (*op. cit.*, p. 5).

[2] Thus an 'agenda for action' drawn up in *Not from Benevolence . . .* (Hobart Paperback 10, 1977), which would have been regarded as extreme only a few years before, reads like a Conservative Manifesto. It included firm control of the money supply, increased competition in the labour market, removal of subsidies, reduction of rent controls, auctioning of planning permissions, charging for services, student loans, cuts in aid, abolition of NEDC, and so on. It also included bold proposals for the reform of social security and a reverse income tax (RIT).

Such worry was, it appears, not unfounded. My intention was to warn the centre-left of the IEA's influence and to stimulate a rational response. I wish I had succeeded.

II. THE FAILURE OF 'MARKET FAILURE'?

A standard argument of the 1960s was that since the market 'failed', in various respects, the government should step in. The Institute may justly argue that the argument has taken rather a battering, partly because it neglected to emphasise a corresponding 'government failure' and partly because of its own shortcomings. In this section I review the theoretical fate of these 'market failures'. Do those once-proud gateways to intervention (uncertainty, ignorance, monopoly, increasing returns to scale, public goods) still admit our passage? I would like to simplify the discussion by invoking two individuals, Blue (broadly representing free market economists and the Institute) and Pink (broadly representing the Fabian view). Developments in economic theory are not, of course, (except in a very subtle sense) 'political': yet some will please Blue and some will please Pink.[3]

Blue has long felt that the general equilibrium competitive model was not quite what he had in mind by 'competition'. This is not surprising, for Pink is able to show that to achieve 'efficiency', let alone optimality, a formidable list of assumptions is necessary. We have to show, using troublesome mathematics, that a competitive equilibrium exists, that there is only one such

[3] It happens that blue is also for a little boy, pink for a girl. The reader is asked to banish this association from his mind.

equilibrium and that it is stable, i.e. that small departures from equilibrium set up negative feedback such that equilibrium is restored. Once the future and the prevalence of uncertainty are taken into account it is further necessary to specify perfect futures markets and perfect markets in contingencies (insurance). Thus modern general equilibrium theory provides a rigorous analysis of economic interrelatedness. But this very complexity is a two-edged sword. Blue will surely welcome those recent refinements that emphasise uncertainty, information costs and disequilibrium, refinements that call into question the very notion of equilibrium itself. For they are closer to the rough, robust, *dynamic* notion of competition favoured by Hayek and Schumpeter than to the old *static* model. On that Smithian notion, competition is characterised not by oscillations around an equilibrium but by experiment, error, adjustment and re-adjustment. It is a process in which the individual tries to better his condition in face of the unplanned and unplannable chaos around him. Modern general equilibrium theory no longer allows us to treat such fundamental features of human life as uncertainty and the search for information merely as examples of 'market failure'.

SCEPTICISM ABOUT EXTERNALITIES

Blue and Pink are, I hope, agreed on the technical analysis of that prominent source of market failure, externalities, or effects (good or bad) on third parties. They differ on its empirical importance and on appropriate solutions. Pink sees externalities under every bed. Blue doubts their importance but (like a Pinkish IEA author, Wilfred Beckerman) favours a pricing solution rather than direct control whenever intervention is held to be necessary. The traditional solution, due to Pigou,[4] is to impose taxes on those who generate external costs and give subsidies to those who generate external benefits—hence Pigovian taxes and subsidies. Most textbooks on welfare economics now discuss the famous 'Coase theorem' (that with well-defined property rights and zero negotiating costs externalities are fully internalised), the difficulties of calculating and implementing the appropriate Pigovian tax-subsidy and even the possibility that an apparently optimal tax could make things worse. The run-of-the-mill economist is now much more sceptical than he was about old-fashioned externalities: this must be very comforting for Blue. The Institute's own scepticism is well illustrated by Cheung *et al.*[5]

Doubts about the possibility of adequate social cost measurement are expressed widely across the profession,[6] not merely by Blues, and one has to admit that progress has been disappointing. Pink is able to acknowledge all of this yet point to the inadequacy of existing mechanisms for dealing with environmental pollution, a public 'bad' (see below) if ever there was one. Pollution fits Pink's case better than that other common form of market failure, resource depletion, for that can (in principle) be settled by the price mechanism itself, as Beckerman insisted.

[4] A. C. Pigou, *Economics of Welfare* (1920). A more detailed discussion is in my essay on Pigou in D. O'Brien (ed.), *Pioneers of Modern Economics,* Macmillan, 1980.

[5] S. Cheung, C. K. Rowley and J. Burton, *The Myth of Social Cost,* Hobart Paper 82, IEA, 1978.

[6] For example, some of the contributors to D. W. Pearce (ed.), *The Valuation of Social Cost*, Allen & Unwin, 1978.

THE 'PUBLIC GOOD' DEBATE

Market failure to provide 'public goods' or to prevent 'public bads' is obviously of intense interest both to Blue and to Pink: again the issue is partly one of empirical claim and counter-claim. Samuelson[7] originally put the public good[8] forward as a polar case: interpreted very strictly it remains an almost empty economic box; even the archetypal case of the lighthouse has been taken apart.[9] Pink would not be foolish enough to justify health and education provision on public good grounds except to a minor degree: defence and law-and-order are his only safe bets and it is rather embarrassing to have to keep emphasising them.

Nevertheless the public good argument remains a threat to Blue if only as the leading species of a large genus, including various local public goods and co-operative enterprises. His obvious recourse is to a Lindahl[10] type of provision whereby everyone pays a 'tax-price' (or contribution to the cost of the public good) equal to his or her marginal valuation: an application of the famous benefit principle of taxation. Yet the

[7] P. A. Samuelson, 'The Pure Theory of Public Expenditure', *Review of Economics and Statistics,* Vol. 36, November 1954.

[8] A public good is a good which if provided at all is provided for everyone and from the benefits of which no-one may (can) be excluded.

[9] R. H. Coase, 'The Lighthouse in Economics', *Journal of Law and Economics*, Vol. 17, October 1974, and A. T. Peacock, *The Economic Analysis of Government*, Martin Robertson, 1979, Chapter 9.

[10] Eric Lindahl, along with Knut Wicksell, Gunnar Myrdal and others, was a member of the Swedish or Stockholm School of economists. For an exposition of the Lindahl solution see his essay, 'Just Taxation: A Positive Solution', reprinted in R. A. Musgrave and A. T. Peacock (eds.), *Classics in the Theory of Public Finance,* International Economic Association, 1958.

underlying theoretical difficulty here, not yet fully resolved, is that of preference revelation. How does one persuade individuals to reveal 'correct' valuations if they know they are going to be used as a basis for taxation? Remarkable progress has been made in this task, in particular the device of 'Grove's mechanisms'[11] (whereby individuals are ingeniously led to reveal true preferences). These mechanisms characteristically attempt to force individuals to pay for the external costs inflicted upon others so there is no longer any advantage in concealing true preferences. However, we are still a long way short of devising rules capable of practical implementation. A successful outcome of this line of highly theoretical inquiry would be intensely gratifying to Blue as true preference revelation seems the only alternative to voluntary coercion through financing by taxes.

If the public good is the leading species of a large genus, local authority provision of goods and services and trade union provision of collective services must be among the constituent population. In both cases Blue has sought to minimise the importance of the truly public element. Thus on local authorities he argues for charges or, better still, private provision even of dustbins and beaches.[12] As for unions he pooh-poohs the truly collective element and, in particular, contests the non-excludability of individuals from negotiated union benefits.[13] For some reason that I do not fully under-

[11] For a recent account see J. R. Green and J. J. Laffont, *Incentives in Public Decision-Making*, North Holland, Amsterdam, 1979.

[12] R. Harris and A. Seldon, *Pricing or Taxing?*, Hobart Paper 71, IEA, 1976.

[13] Lord Robbins *et al., Trade Unions: Public Goods or Public 'Bads'?*, IEA Readings 17, 1978.

stand, Blue has decided to put Mancur Olson,[14] one of the leading theorists of collective action, into a distinguished rogues' gallery which already exhibits Samuelson, Arrow and Keynes.

Externalities and public goods are very closely related, both being examples of 'jointness'. One embarrassing feature of jointness for Blue is that a pursuit of narrow self-interest on the part of each individual might lead to worse outcomes than under a 'co-operative' solution. This type of case has been extensively discussed by Sen,[15] Hirsch[16] and by the present author,[17] and it turns out, interestingly enough, that (for efficiency) each should behave *as though* concerned for the good of all. Adam Smith's famous invisible hand then no longer works. Pink believes that, partly because of pollution, these 'prisoners' dilemma' scenarios will become more common rather than less. If he is a Titmuss[18]-type Pink (the sort of person referred to by Blues as a Titmouse), he believes that a more extensive use of the market and of the self-interest motive could atrophy those co-operative instincts on which we shall come increasingly to rely. One such instinct is the altruistic one and I sug-

[14] M. Olson, *The Logic of Collective Action,* Harvard University Press, Cambridge, Mass., 1965.

[15] A. K. Sen, 'Behaviour and the Concept of Preference', *Economica,* May 1973.

[16] F. Hirsch, *Social Limits to Growth,* Routledge and Kegan Paul, 1977.

[17] D. A. Collard, *Altruism and Economy*, Martin Robertson, 1978.

[18] Titmuss had used blood donation as a peg on which to hang a general proposition about 'gift-relationships' versus the market. (R. M. Titmuss, *The Gift Relationship*, Allen & Unwin, 1970.)

gested in my *Tract* that 'collective provision is the most efficient way of incorporating unselfish feelings'.

AGREEMENT ON MONOPOLIES

Pink and Blue are agreed that monopolies, the next form of market failure to be considered, are a bad thing. The Institute's position on monopoly has been consistently critical[19] (especially when the monopoly was a state one). In this respect it has differed sharply from intellectually less distinguished pressure-groups of the Right. Recent upward shifts in the measurement of social loss due to monopoly power have strengthened the hands of critics of monopoly. On the other hand, both Pink and Blue are going to have to rethink their positions as a result of theoretical advances in what I would call a neo-Schumpeterian direction, for example, the suggestion of Dasgupta and Stiglitz[20] that market structure should be treated as given but determined by demand, costs and technology. On this interpretation, to 'control' monopoly price/output behaviour is merely to treat the symptom of an underlying condition.

One of the key assumptions noted earlier was the absence of economies of large-scale production. Now manufacturing industry seems to display roughly constant and perhaps very slightly increasing returns. Does the intellectual apparatus on which the market

[19] A recent example is the study by T. J. Gough and T. W. Taylor, *The Building Society Price Cartel*, Hobart Paper 83, IEA, 1979. As I noted of the Institute in my Fabian Tract, 'its careful descriptions of, and attacks upon, restrictive trade practices have been particularly impressive'.

[20] P. Dasgupta and J. Stiglitz, 'Industrial Structure and the Nature of Innovative Activity', *Economic Journal*, Vol. 90, June 1980.

economist depends apply, then, only to small-scale activity? Is Blue the victim of a small business mentality? If things have to be done on a large scale in conditions of (roughly) constant returns, with approximate pricing policies, does it matter very much whether they are run by the Chairman of ICI or the Chairman of a nationalised industry? Blue's response must refer to the economics of bureaucracy (discussed below): for the strength of private bureaucracy is limited by the extent of the market. Even very large corporations can go bankrupt. But are there similar limits to the strength of public bureaucracies?

Looking back over this discussion of 'market failure', Blue will emphasise the sterility of the static general equilibrium 'ideal', the integral rôle of uncertainty and ignorance, the spontaneous internalisation of externalities, and the possibility of mechanisms that reveal incentives for public goods. Pink will emphasise the lack of adequate proofs of optimality, the prevalence of jointness, and the potential self-destructiveness of self-interest. At this point I introduce the third actor in this drama, Blink, an uncertain, nervous character who finds the whole thing very difficult. Is theory Pink or is it Blue? It is, of course, neither: it is just theory. At this point Blue asks Blink to have a look at the literature on government failure.

III. THE SUCCESS OF 'GOVERNMENT FAILURE'?

Modern writing on the economic theory of politics quite rightly criticises a methodological lapse in some of the earlier criticisms of the market. It seemed that one had only to highlight some aspect of market failure in order to demonstrate the advisability of government intervention. Thanks to the work of Niskanen[21] and others, popularised by the Institute, we are now more acutely aware than we were of 'government failure'. The central contribution of this line of argument, warmly embraced by Blue, is that the actions of all individuals (not only entrepreneurs and consumers but politicians and bureaucrats as well) may be analysed as though they were maximising their own utility. Politicians and bureaucrats are not saints: they will pursue their own interests as they perceive them. There is no guarantee that their interests will be society's interest (whatever that might be): to ensure this result, wise institutions have to be devised.[22]

ECONOMICS OF BUREAUCRACY

In a sense none of this is new. The man in the street has for a long time sensed that the bureaucrat is no saint. But, if not, what is he maximising? In answering this question the new literature has had less success than in its broad methodological assertion that he must be maximising *something*. Niskanen favours the size of the 'bureau' as the main measureable component because it reveals a close correlation between remuneration, prestige, power and so on. Alan Peacock has emphasised 'on-the-job leisure'. Interest in the policy objectives themselves is not ruled out: it is merely that they play

[21] W. A. Niskanen, *Bureaucracy: Servant or Master?,* Hobart Paperback 5, IEA, 1973. Also G. Tullock, *The Vote Motive,* Hobart Paperback 9, IEA, 1976.

[22] Academic commentators are also busy maximising their utilities: it is left to competition in the world of ideas to sort the wheat from the chaff.

a minor rôle. The appropriate assumption depends a great deal on the level of bureaucracy at which one is working—permanent secretary or junior official. It is easy to understand why junior officials are averse to risk, for superiors and public alike are interested only when something goes wrong. As the penalty for mistakes can be severe (in terms of promotion prospects, etc.), there is a strong incentive to stick to the routines even where they offend common-sense and the interests of the client. For more senior officials the rewards for successful departure from the old routines can be large, especially if they lead to a bigger empire. Niskanen's hypothesis applies more readily to the senior creative bureaucrat than to the minor official. Bureaucrats no more aim at the public interest than do businessmen.

The economics of bureaucracy is merely part of the new 'economic theory of politics' which my generation first encountered in the work of Buchanan and Tullock[23] and in Anthony Downs.[24] By the late 1960s many of us were using this material in teaching. All the main participants, party politicians, voters and bureaucrats, try to maximise utility. Party politicians wish to maximise votes or at least stay in office. Voters balance the benefits of promised policies against expected 'tax-prices'; even their decision on whether or not to vote is made on a rational calculus. Bureaucrats maximise their budgets. The upshot depends on the constitution. On simple majority voting with a two-party system it may be shown that policies converge on the preferences

[23] J. M. Buchanan and G. Tullock, *The Calculus of Consent*, Ann Arbor, Michigan, 1962.

[24] A. Downs, *The Economic Theory of Democracy*, Harper and Row, New York, 1965.

of the 'median' voter. They are then carried out by the bureaucrat. In this simple model the politicians and the bureaucrat are merely ciphers. In real systems there is a thick, sometimes impenetrable, fog between the voter and his public servants. Not only does he lack sufficient information to be precise about his political calculus, but there are many 'issues' to be weighed together and his participation is not by referendum but by parliamentary representatives. It is under the cover of this fog that the Niskanen-type bureaucrat can function.

There is surely, replies Pink, an equally effective fog in the private sector which enables the opportunist producer to grow fat at the consumer's expense. But the 'invisible hand' is supposed to check these opportunities so that, in the end, the producer is led to serve the general interest. To some degree a similar invisible hand is at work in the public sector. A bureaucrat bent on a Rake's Progress would presumably be dismissed (or at least transferred) by his Minister. Similarly, a Minister whose policies were persistently electorally unpopular would presumably be dismissed by his Prime Minister; and a persistently unpopular government would eventually be dismissed by the electorate. One has only to list these mechanisms, however, to appreciate their weaknesses.

A SENSE OF DUTY?

Pink would still wish to insist, I think, that a sense of 'duty' must play a part in all this. Blue scoffs at duty as an efficient social device outside of the family unit (and, indeed, even inside!).[25] But a whole range of

[25] I. Papps, *For Love or Money?*, Hobart Paper 86, IEA, 1980, has drawn upon the now famous writings of the Chicago School on the economics of the family, marriage, etc.

human behaviour, from the regular voter in a non-marginal constituency to the tireless and dedicated public servant, can be better explained by public-spiritedness than by a rational calculation of costs and benefits. As it would be unwise to rely heavily on this phenomenon, so it would be foolish to denigrate it. Lack of use leads to atrophy.

Duty apart, the response to government failure, as to market failure, is the clever devising of suitable rewards and punishments. Though in its details this is a matter for specialists in management, the broad outlines are obvious enough: the task is to ensure more 'accountability'. In local government this means more genuine decentralisation but with local revenue, not merely the creation of extra layers. If, as seems likely, this led to wider variety, the hugely discontented, as in Tiebout's[26] model, might then find it worth while to move to another area where the mix of services and local taxes was more to their liking. Such an outcome would be more in accord with the benefit principle whose Blue-ish colour has already been commented upon.

Central government cannot, except by migration, be dealt with on the same principle. Neither is the plebiscite an effective device for accountability whenever the issues are inter-related (as in a complete taxation-public expenditure package): for a bundle of policies has then to be considered together in the manner of a political platform. 'Log-rolling' (political dealing in which support is exchanged) is useful[27] in making sure that policies

[26] In Tiebout's model the individual votes with his feet. (C. Tiebout, 'A Pure Theory of Local Expenditures', *Journal of Political Economy* (1956).)

[27] Chapter V of Tullock, *op. cit.*

reflect the balance of preferences in the legislature but not necessarily the balance of preferences in the electorate at large.

WEIGHING THE COSTS OF GOVERNMENT AND MARKET 'FAILURE'

Pink has to concede, I think, that bureaucratic expansion and operational inefficiency will continue to characterise public provision to some degree. Such 'government failure' does not, of course, imply either that a service should not be provided at all or that it should not be provided publicly. It could very well be 'worth' having public provision to some degree *in spite of* bureaucratic failure, just as it might be worth having a private market in spite of market failure. One of the more routine tasks of the economist is to provide politically neutral advice on which institutional structure is most appropriate.

Broadly, Blink's position would be that when the welfare loss due to government failure is less than the welfare loss due to market failure, government provision should be chosen. To help make this point, consider a simple class of private goods. Let market failure take the form of ignoring an externality: let government failure take the form of excessive expansion. Hence there is 'failure' in both camps. Both methods of provision are inferior to *either* ideal public provision (where there is no bureaucratic excess) or to private provision with an appropriate Pigovian tax. But let us suppose that neither of these is attainable. It then becomes necessary to strike a balance of welfare losses due to externalities and welfare losses due to bureaucratic expansion. The existence of 'government failure' is no more a case for the market than 'market failure' is a case for public provision.

All mechanisms are characterised by 'failure' of some sort: the thing is to be clever enough to design our institutions so as to achieve a second-best. Blink is more likely to achieve this by examining cases than are Blue and Pink in their debating chamber.

IV. WHOSE SOCIAL WELFARE FUNCTION?

Our discussion of market failure and government failure has been in terms of 'efficiency', which requires only the harmless axiom that more is preferred to less. Equity is quite a different matter requiring us to judge some distributions of income as preferable to others. One person's view about equity is as good as another's: it embodies a personal value-judgement. Blue's value-judgements and Pink's are equally valid.

An important advance of the last decade or so in economic analysis is agreement about a convenient technical way of discussing and comparing judgements about distribution. Thus Atkinson[28] was able to show that a wide variety of distributional preferences may be captured conceptually in a single index, the degree of aversion to inequality. This enables economists with different attitudes to income distribution to agree on a way of measuring these differences and to test how sensitive their policy recommendations are to them.

There is an important distinction to be drawn, I think, between IEA authors' views of distribution and the view of some philosophers of the Right. Let us refer

[28] A. B. Atkinson, 'On the Measurement of Inequality', *Journal of Economic Theory*, 2, 1970.

to these as Blue and True Blue. Blue's social welfare function[29] may usefully be characterised as: maximise real income, subject to (i) no-one falling below a prescribed poverty line[30] and (ii) economic liberalism. He emphasises poverty rather than equality. True Blue, however, raises the fundamental distinction (to use Jeremy Bentham's language) between Agenda and Non-Agenda: what the state should and should not do. Is distribution on the agenda for action or is it not?

Blue has never asked, as far as I recall, for distribution to be removed from the agenda. Nozick's view[31] that distribution has no place is implicitly rejected. His argument, roughly, is that individuals are entitled to their income from earnings or to unearned income built up by their ancestors and freely transferred to them. The entitlement is theirs and no-one else's, certainly not the state's. We have no business to interfere with income distribution. The only sorts of redistribution permitted are voluntary: any coercive redistribution conflicts with natural liberty.

This approach contrasts very sharply with Rawls's view,[32] based on social contract theory, that justice

[29] A social welfare function is a social 'ordering' or 'ranking' of possible alternative allocations of resources.

[30] A convenient list of IEA Studies on the Economics of Social Policy is to be found at Appendix F to R. Harris and A. Seldon, *Over-Ruled on Welfare*, Hobart Paperback 13, IEA, 1979.

[31] R. Nozick, *Anarchy, State and Utopia*, Blackwell, Oxford, 1974.

[32] J. Rawls, *A Theory of Justice*, Harvard University Press, 1971. The discussion of justice in Rawls's book is long and complex and includes a case for the priority of liberty but social scientists have tended to fasten upon the maxi-min principle, whereby the policy-maker attempts to maximise the income of the poorest individual.

requires us to maximise the income of the least-well-off. Like most principles, these contrasting rules lose their sharp edges when it comes to cases. Nozick's principle could, in practice, accommodate some non-voluntary redistribution for the sake of correcting earlier unjust transfers of income/wealth. And once the effects of compulsory redistribution on incentives and savings are taken into account, Rawls's principle is nothing like as egalitarian as it first appears.

IEA economists are prepared to redistribute income/wealth to ensure a minimum standard of income. It is a judgement which Pink and Blue may argue about but which nevertheless implies a place on the agenda. But Blue also wishes to stress economic liberalism. Obviously there are potential difficulties here, for a programme to prevent poverty would require 'voluntary coercion' in order to overcome the free-rider problem: even so, the principle of economic liberalism is of some help here for it stresses cash transfers[33] rather than transfers in kind. One would imagine that when it came to questions of efficient output (as contrasted with distribution) there would be no such difficulty. Yet theorists, basing their discussion of efficiency on the Pareto-principle (that a sufficient condition for economic welfare to increase is that someone is made better off without anyone being made worse off) have noticed possible clashes with liberalism. In particular Sen[34] has taken a pretty innocent-looking definition of liberalism and has shown that it contradicts the Pareto-principle. Sen favours throwing out the latter. Others, like

[33] See the discussion of transfers in kind in Collard, *op. cit.*, 1978.

[34] A. K. Sen, 'The Impossibility of a Paretian Liberal', *Journal of Political Economy*, January 1970.

Rowley and Peacock,[35] have quarrelled with his definition of liberalism. My own view, strengthened by the fanciful examples often used (e.g. the attitudes of the lascivious reader and the prude to *Lady Chatterley's Lover*), is that Sen's 'impossibility theorem' is of limited relevance to the allocation of resources. If so, the much reviled Pareto principle still has a part to play.

Modern thinking on the possibility of rational social choice is closely associated with the work of Arrow.[36] Unfortunately, Blue has tended to treat his work as hostile. Arrow was not a frustrated planner, trying to establish a social welfare function and failing in the attempt. He showed that *any* method of basing social choice on individual valuations was in some way unacceptable. Blue's free-market mechanism is just as vulnerable to the proposition as any other mechanism. How can this be? Because market processes violate the principle of 'unlimited domain', i.e. they do not work over all allocations of income/wealth but only over Pareto-inferior or Pareto-superior ones. I think I am right in saying that the market mechanism violates none of the other Arrovian requirements:[37] it is transitive, it provides a positive association between individual and social orderings, it satisfies the Pareto-principle, it is

[35] C. K. Rowley and A. T. Peacock, *Welfare Economics: A Liberal Restatement*, Martin Robertson, 1975, Chapter 5.

[36] K. J. Arrow, *Social Choice and Individual Values*, Wiley, 1951, 2nd Edition, 1963.

[37] The other requirements are that it is transitive (violated by cyclical majorities), that it satisfies the Pareto-principle (violated by non-voluntary redistribution), that it is neither imposed (by planners) nor dictatorial, and that it is 'independent of irrelevant alternatives' (violated by many voting systems).

neither imposed nor dictatorial, and it is independent of irrelevant alternatives. But, if Arrow's theorem holds, the market cannot escape and it is indeed caught by 'unlimited domain' just as the planner is caught by 'imposition', i.e. imposing his own preferences as planner. Blue and Pink are tarred with the same Arrovian brush. The difference is that Blue does not much mind violating 'unlimited domain' while Pink does not much mind violating 'imposition'.

V. THE COUNTER-REVOLUTION IN MACRO-ECONOMICS

For economists of my generation who learned their Keynesian macro-economics in the 1950s, the shift in intellectual climate in the last 25 years has been dramatic, even traumatic. Far from being a lasting 'revolution' or 'general theory', it is now claimed that Keynesian economics was merely an episode, like the brilliant but short-lived Physiocratic episode in the 18th century. This demise has been accompanied by the rise of 'monetarism'. It so happens that Keynesianism has Pink associations and Monetarism Blue associations, though the links are by no means essential: there could be a Keynesian economy in which effective demand was manipulated through private firms or a Monetarist economy with a strong welfare state and high taxes.

THE NEW MACRO-ECONOMICS

In its earlier years Institute economists had little to say about macro-economics. Neither did I give it much space in my (1968) Fabian Tract, remarking *en passant* that

> 'in so far as investment leads to cyclical instability we have learned (successfully) how to manipulate monetary and fiscal policies so as to maintain relative stability at (near) full employment'.[38]

In more recent years the Institute has been prominent in publicising the current disillusionment with Keynesian economics, a disillusionment carried to extremes in the rational expectations literature which argues that controls cannot work if economic agents' (buyers' and sellers') expectations are based on the same (correct) anticipations as the government's. The initial stages of the counter-revolution in the 1960s were exegetical[39] only, but by the 1970s the Institute was presenting the policy recommendations of Hayek[40] and of Friedman,[41] and Buchanan *et al.* were able to take a dismal view of *The Consequences of Mr Keynes*.[42] From the Institute's point of view the new macro-economics is attractive both politically and philosophically.

There are many strands in the current debate and the Institute has, not unreasonably from its own pedagogical point of view, picked on one of them, an amalgam of

[38] *Op. cit.*, p. 5.

[39] Axel Leijonhufvud's work was popularised by the Institute in Occasional Paper No. 30, *Keynes and the Classics*, 1969.

[40] F. A. Hayek, *A Tiger by the Tail* (compiled by Sudha Shenoy), Hobart Paperback 4, 1972; *Full Employment at Any Price?*, Occasional Paper 45, 1975.

[41] Milton Friedman, *The Counter-Revolution in Monetary Theory*, Occasional Paper 33, 1970; *Monetary Correction*, Occasional Paper 41, 1974; *Unemployment versus Inflation?*, Occasional Paper 44, 1975.

[42] J. M. Buchanan, J. Burton and R. E. Wagner, *The Consequences of Mr Keynes*, Hobart Paper 78, 1978.

'Friedmanism' and rational expectations. Another strand, at least as respectable academically, to which it has not given attention, is the literature that starts from Clower and tries to derive optimal control rules given restrictions on choice by households and firms (rationing).[43] Monetarists believe that control of the money supply enables policy-makers to control the rate of inflation without (given rational expectations) affecting real economic variables. If rational expectations do not work perfectly the state is, after all, able to control real economic variables. And if you are going to use macro-economic instruments you might as well use all the information that becomes available rather than simply impose a rule like Friedman's. An economic system which is capable of producing rapid inflation and/or high unemployment cries out for a better control system than any used so far. The task of post-Keynesian macro-economics is to add other instruments to the simple one of effective demand. This strand of argument lacks glamour and simplicity, so it has less appeal to financial journalists and publicists; but it does seem to be the best way forward.

It is a pity that macro-economic discussion has concentrated so much on the Phillips curve (the 'trade-off' between unemployment and money wage inflation), which emphasised the Keynesian control of effective demand alone. Yet Keynes had himself analysed the need for extra controls, such as post-war credits, at full-employment in *How to Pay for the War*, and Pigou argued that

[43] E.g. J. Muellbauer and R. Portes, 'Macroeconomic Models with Quantity Rationing', *Economic Journal*, Vol. 88, December 1978, pp. 788-822.

> 'if the authorities continue to strive after the goal they originally set themselves, they must so act as to push aggregate money income always higher and higher . . . the only way in which that risk may be obviated is by restraint on the part of wage-earners in pressing for increases in money wage rates.'[44]

Hayek would, of course, see any such policy as a major step on the Road to Serfdom, and it has to be admitted that incomes policies have not been triumphantly successful. Yet is it hubris to feel, with Keynes, that the answer lies in cleverness rather than masochism?

> 'It is, in the strictest sense, an economic problem, or to express it better, as suggesting a blend of economic theory with the art of statesmanship, a problem of political economy, . . . it is appropriate to the case that the remedy should be found in something which can fairly be called a *device*.'[45]

Such a device would earn great prizes and ingenious, though probably impracticable, schemes have been put forward, notably by Professor James E. Meade. One alternative basis for a successful device would be the isolation of bargaining over relative wages (in terms of an average or *numéraire* wage) from the determination of the absolute money wage. But we are only beginning to understand how this might be done.

VI. CONCLUSION

I see two principal features in the development of economic theory in the last twenty years or so. The first

[44] A. C. Pigou, *A Study in Public Finance,* 3rd Edn., Macmillan, 1947.

[45] J. M. Keynes, 'The Means to Prosperity', in *Collected Writings,* Vol. IX, Macmillan, 1972, p. 336.

is to do with increasing complexity and an increasing awareness of interdependence and has profound implications for political economy. It springs from the development of the internal logic of economics and is in that sense a scientific development. Add to that its obscurity and it brings no obvious political comfort to anyone. The Institute has not emphasised this and one would not expect it to. The second is the comfort offered to market economists by the emergent analysis of collective choice and 'government failure' at the micro-economic level and of monetarism at the macro-economic level. The Institute has taken full advantage of this feature and I do not blame it for making hay while the sun shines. If it tried to be neutral it would become dull and we should all be the worse for that.

Chapter VII

PRICING AND PUBLIC CHOICE IN SOCIAL WELFARE

Ken Judge

Senior Research Fellow,
University of Kent at Canterbury

The Author

KEN JUDGE is a Senior Research Fellow, and Assistant Director of the Personal Social Services Research Unit, University of Kent at Canterbury. Previously he was a Lecturer in Social Policy at the University of Bristol (1974-79) and the Civil Service College (1979-80). He is Editor of the *Journal of Social Policy*, and his publications include *Rationing Social Services* (1978); *Pricing the Social Services* (1980); *Charging for Social Care* (1980).

Pricing and Public Choice in Social Welfare

INTRODUCTION

Most traditional studies of social policy have emphasised market failure and government beneficence as central features of alleviating social needs and problems in the modern Welfare State. In contrast, the IEA has drawn attention to the contradictions of representative democracies and the propensity of governments to overload themselves, and has advocated the substitution of the efficiency-inducing power of markets and prices in place of bureaucratic and political decision-making. The purpose of this Chapter is to examine some of the strengths and weaknesses of the two main sets of ideas promoted by the IEA in social policy: public choice explanations of the growth of government; and the use of consumer charges to provide and allocate social services.

PUBLIC CHOICE IN THE POLITICAL MARKET

The economic study of political behaviour and social choice has generated a substantial literature in recent years which is generally referred to as *public choice*.[1]

[1] Dennis C. Mueller, *Public Choice*, Cambridge University Press, Cambridge, 1979; and James M. Buchanan *et al.*, *The Economics of Politics*, IEA Readings 18, Institute of Economic Affairs, 1978.

The theories which have been generated have descriptive and prescriptive aspects and they address questions associated with both the demand and supply of public policies. On balance, however, the IEA has highlighted the observable supply-side features of public choice. In short, IEA Papers have emphasised the extent to which politicians and bureaucrats manipulate the instruments of government to stimulate an excessive supply of collective goods and services. These ideas are elaborated in a little more detail below, but the reader should be warned that scant justice can be done to their sophistication in a few paragraphs.

To start with, it is helpful to think of a market for public policies which is analogous to the familiar market for private goods and services. Some citizens then have preferences for packages of collective services and the tax prices associated with them which they can transmit into demands. Following Professor Albert Breton[2] we can use the term *coercion* to describe the dissatisfaction felt by the citizen who thinks the government is not providing the correct policies at the right prices. This is an important concept because, if the citizen feels strongly enough, it provides a *rationale* for engaging in political action to modify the policy.

But public policies are supplied by politicians, bureaucrats and other public employees only partly in response to citizens' demands, because many of them have a vested interest in the growth of public agencies together with the means to achieve such objectives. One of the best examples of this phenomenon is the political-business cycle in which governments make use of the

[2] Albert Breton, *The Economic Theory of Representative Government*, Macmillan, 1974.

fiscal instruments at their disposal to try and manipulate the results of elections.[3] An equilibrium between demand and supply in the political market can, of course, be established only within an institutional framework which reflects the critical and shifting power relationships between, say, suppliers and consumers and politicians and tax-payers within society, but certain characteristic features of representative democracy can introduce distortions. Some of the most notable examples are *full-line supply*, *log-rolling*, the *median voter theorem* and *fiscal illusion*.

FULL-LINE SUPPLY OF GOVERNMENT 'BUNDLE' CONFLICTING WITH PUBLIC PREFERENCE

The *raison d'être* of representative democracies is to provide the community, through elected representatives, not with one particular policy but with a bundle of public policies. When citizens vote in an election they face a choice between two or more competing *sets* of policies. As a result of this aspect of the institutional framework the elector is forced, in a sense, to accept the full supply of policies offered by the chosen candidate or party. Because of this phenomenon, called *full-line supply*, Professor Breton argues that

> 'politicians have the freedom to supply a number of public policies which are at variance with some of the preferences even of the citizens who support them'.[4]

To accept this view, one needs to reflect that the citizen/elector may choose to support a candidate/party which

[3] Bruno S. Frey, *Modern Political Economy*, Martin Robertson, Oxford, 1978.

[4] Breton, *op. cit.*, p. 50.

promises to provide policies upon which he places a high value regardless of whether other policies which are included in the full supply have a positive or negative value to him. Alternatively, as Professor Breton puts it,

> 'a citizen will choose among candidates the one who offers the bundle of policies with the highest expected utility even though this may imply accepting policies he does not like'.[5]

LOG-ROLLING: TRADING IN THE POLITICAL MARKET

Variations in preference intensities between policy issues provides opportunities for participants in the policy process to engage in *log-rolling* or vote trading. In a society with three persons (*A, B* and *C*) having to decide about two public issues (*X* and *Y*), *B* may favour policy *X* and *C* support policy *Y*, but *A* is opposed to both. If each issue were decided separately by majority rule both would fail because in each there are more voters who would lose than gain. In these circumstances *B* and *C* would gain by supporting each other to ensure the passage of the two issues. In this sense log-rolling is the political equivalent of exchange in private goods. It is important to realise, however, that log-rolling may impose external costs on third-parties. In this example, costs will have been imposed on *A* by *B* and *C*, and Professor Gordon Tullock has argued[6] that, in certain circumstances, the operation of majority rule voting procedures together with log-rolling can lead to the

[5] *Ibid.*

[6] Gordon Tullock, *The Vote Motive*, Hobart Paperback 9, IEA, 1976.

approval of policies that have adverse consequences for the entire community.

Log-rolling is a common phenomenon in all democratic political systems and, although it is frequently concealed from public scrutiny, it can have considerable influence on eventual outcomes in policy through its influence on, say, Cabinet decision-making. The late R. H. S. Crossman, for example, records in his *Diaries* the following conversation with Roy Jenkins, then Chancellor of the Exchequer, in June 1968:

> '"Now, Dick, let's be practical. If I agree with you about postponing the decision on Social Services cuts for a week will you give me your full support on Fulton?". "Yes", I said, "if you will support me on Lord's reform as well". And that, roughly speaking, was the deal we came to'.[7]

THE MEDIAN VOTER THEOREM AND WINNING COALITIONS

The median voter is said to be the one occupying the middle ground of any particular issue; that is to say, midway in the range of opinions or values expressed about any policy. The *median voter theorem* simply states that if a number of voters with different views on an issue choose by majority voting, the outcome will be the optimum of the median voter.[8] Although this is a very simple proposition, it is of considerable significance in the economics of politics because of the tendency of modern political parties to adopt the position of the median voter in an attempt to build a winning coalition and obtain, or remain in, power. The

[7] Richard Crossman, *The Diaries of a Cabinet Minister*, Vol. 3' Hamish Hamilton and Jonathan Cape, 1977, p. 98.

[8] Tullock, *op. cit.*

result is that winning parties usually commit themselves to some spending policies which have low priority by reference to their own ideological values.

FISCAL ILLUSION AND DEFICIT FINANCING

It has long been popularly held that governments are never short of ideas about how to spend money but are constrained by their unwillingness to be seen increasing taxation.[9] Fiscal illusion refers to all of the relatively invisible ways in which government is able to raise additional finance.[10] One of the most important examples is deficit financing legitimised by the adoption of Keynesian economic policies after the Second World War.

At its simplest the Keynesian policy rule required the creation of budget deficits to stimulate aggregate demand during a recession and budget surpluses to stabilise demand when the economy was in danger of overheating. Throughout the post-war period, therefore, the manipulation of public expenditure, usually in an upward direction, became one of the chief instruments available to government in the pursuit of economic prosperity and social progress. But in recent years a growing body of monetarist and public choice literature has drawn attention to the adverse economic consequence of the way in which Keynesian economic ideas have been implemented by politicians. Professor J. M. Buchanan and his collaborators, in particular,

[9] Alan Peacock and Jack Wiseman, *The Growth of Public Expenditure in the United Kingdom*, 2nd Edn., George Allen & Unwin, 1967.

[10] D. R. Morgan, *Over-Taxation by Inflation*, Hobart Paper 72, 2nd Edn., IEA, 1977.

have drawn attention to the increased willingness of governments to sanction budget deficits rather than surpluses.

> 'The grafting of Keynesian economics onto the fabric of a political democracy has wrought a significant revision in the underlying fiscal constitution. . . . the perceived cost of government will generally be lower than the real cost because of the deficit financing. As a consequence, there will also be a relative increase in the size of the government sector in the economy.'[11]

CRITICISMS OF PUBLIC CHOICE

Public choice theory has much to offer to any serious student of government but in some respects it is both simplistic and restrictive in its approach. Let me draw attention to two of these weaknesses.

First, the crude individualistic assumptions about human behaviour upon which the public choice approach rests are anathema to many non-economists. In particular, the simplistic assumptions about the motivations of, say, civil servants do more harm than good. Professor Buchanan has suggested that it is less important to develop testable propositions than to develop sophisticated but plausible theories. If that is so, we require a much more realistic appraisal of the perceptions of motivations and rewards held by all public employees. A good start could be made by fully incorporating the work of Professors Herbert Simon[12] and

[11] J. M. Buchanan, J. Burton and R. E. Wagner, *The Consequences of Mr Keynes*, Hobart Paper 78, IEA, 1978, p. 23.

[12] Herbert A. Simon, 'Rational Decision Making in Business Organisations', *American Economic Review*, Vol. 69, No. 4, September 1979, pp. 493-513.

Harvey Leibenstein[13] into public choice theorising. Their work demonstrates, for example, that bureaucratic behaviour is constrained by rules and social norms which severely limit the pursuit of crude self-interest.

Second, one of the most important factors in explaining the development of public policy, but which has been neglected, is that of political advertising, defined as:

> 'the promotion of a particular product, idea or issue through the provision of publicly available information by politicians, bureaucrats, producers or ordinary citizens who have the intention of either altering or sustaining the supply of policies by governments'.[14]

Politicians will not totally ignore citizens' preferences because they will want to maximise their chances of re-election. This constraint provides an incentive for politicians, public employees, pressure-groups and individual citizens to try to alter the preferences of the electorate. The result is that large numbers of individuals and groups are involved in producing information for public consumption which increases demands for collective goods and services.

Examples are widespread. Private sector producers like drug companies are active in public relations in order to raise the demand for their products supplied to the NHS. Politicians, keen to improve their ministerial reputations, make speeches which are reported in

[13] Harvey Leibenstein, 'A Branch of Economics is Missing: Micro-Micro Theory', *Journal of Economic Literature*, Vol. XVII, June 1979, pp. 477-502.

[14] Ken Judge and Roger Hampson, 'Political advertising and the growth of social welfare expenditures', *International Journal of Social Economics,* Vol. 7, No. 2, 1980, pp. 61-92.

the media. Promotional groups and professional associations are active in pursuit of their special interests. The reports of official commissions and inquiries advocate the improved and more extensive use of government services; and so on in both the public and private sectors.

CHARGES TO FINANCE WELFARE[15]

One of the ways in which IEA economists would limit the coercive power of government is through constitutional innovation,[16] but their more traditional argument is in favour of reviving the use of the price mechanism in the Welfare State and other parts of the public sector to redistribute decision-making power from politicians and bureaucrats to citizens and consumers. In advocating these ideas IEA publications have developed a clear set of principles, based upon economic theory, with which to analyse the Welfare State.

First, they reject the notion that the traditional social services are primarily or substantially public goods which can be financed on those grounds out of general taxation. The only major programmes which fall into this category are defence, law and order, and external relations.

Second, it is suggested that the supposed external benefits associated with social services either do not exist or that there are so many of them they have little

[15] This section is adapted from my article, 'Resource Allocation in the Welfare State: Bureaucrats or Prices', *Journal of Social Policy,* Vol. 8, Part 3, July 1979, pp. 371-82.

[16] H. Geoffrey Brennan and James M. Buchanan, *Monopoly in Money and Inflation*, Hobart Paper 88, IEA, 1981.

practical meaning. Consequently, it is assumed that services in kind such as health care, housing, education and personal social services yield largely separable private benefits. Or, at the very least, that the onus of producing evidence is on those who claim, with much passion and little rational argument, that the supposed external benefits justify seemingly limitless subsidies without proper consideration of their opportunity costs.

Third, it is argued that the concept of 'merit goods' is devoid of true economic meaning and that it is merely an ethereal smokescreen designed to hide the meddlesome paternalism of bureaucrats and politicians.

Fourth, it is generally implied that the transaction costs of non-market resource allocation by government usually exceed those associated with pricing. In his discussion of externalities, for example, Arthur Seldon suggests that, even if they

> 'could be identified and measured, the cost of transferring the subsidies from everyone to everyone else would in the end exceed the benefits'.[17]

In essence, therefore, the IEA case rests on the critical assumption that most social services provide substantial private benefits to more or less easily identifiable individuals and that an increased use of charges, in conjunction with transfer payments in cash to achieve the objectives of income maintenance, would produce considerable benefits for society at large. Charges, it is argued, are a logical consequence of the recognition and adoption of the benefit principle; they result in a more efficient use of resources by signalling preferences to

[17] Arthur Seldon, *Charge*, Temple Smith, London, 1977, p. 53.

decision-makers; they promote consumer choice, individual liberty and human freedom; and they provide additional finance for undernourished services like education and health since people will be prepared to pay more in prices than in taxes because of the more direct relationship between the perceived costs and benefits of their own consumption.

THE CHALLENGE TO ORTHODOXY

The IEA has published almost 300 Hobart and other Papers and books. As many of them are concerned with some aspect of social policy, however, it is impossible to refer to more than a few, but I should mention education and health because these are probably the two areas where IEA authors have mounted their strongest challenge to the established orthodoxy.

Professors A. T. Peacock and Jack Wiseman,[18] Professor A. R. Prest,[19] Professor Peacock and A. J. Culyer,[20] Alan Maynard,[21] and Professor M. A. Crew and Dr Alistair Young[22] have all recognised that government grants have a necessary place in financing education, but they claim that the discipline of the price mechanism will result in considerable improvements in its organisation and mode of provision. It is believed,

[18] Alan T. Peacock and Jack Wiseman, *Education for Democrats*, Hobart Paper 25, IEA, 1964.

[19] A. R. Prest, *Financing University Education*, Occasional Paper 12, IEA, 1966.

[20] Alan T. Peacock and Anthony J. Culyer, *Economic Aspects of Student Unrest*, Occasional Paper 26, IEA, 1969.

[21] Alan Maynard, *Experiment with Choice in Education*, Hobart Paper 64, IEA, 1975.

[22] Michael A. Crew and Alistair Young, *Paying by Degrees*, Hobart Paper 75, IEA, 1977.

for example, that the use of education vouchers for compulsory schooling will promote genuine participation, maximise curriculum choice and encourage efficiency through competition. Similarly, more reliance on loans to finance higher education will encourage universities and polytechnics to become more flexible and responsive to student demands as well as reflecting the high private rate of return accruing to individual recipients of advanced education. Professors D. S. Lees[23] and J. M. Buchanan[24] and Arthur Seldon[25] are all equally critical of the largely collective financing of the National Health Service (NHS). They suggest that the institutional framework of British health care encourages people as patients to demand more than they are willing to pay for as citizens. Not surprisingly, the solution they advocate is a substantial extension of the use of private insurance so as to maximise individual freedom of choice. Other IEA authors have advocated that the neo-classical economic theory relevant to education and health is just as applicable to many other spheres, for example, housing in both the private and public sectors,[26]

[23] D. S. Lees, *Health through Choice,* Hobart Paper 14, 1961, reprinted in Ralph Harris (ed.), *Freedom or Free-for-All?*, Collected Hobart Papers, Vol. 3, IEA, 1965.

[24] James M. Buchanan, *The Inconsistencies of the National Health Service,* Occasional Paper 7, IEA, 1965.

[25] Arthur Seldon, *After the NHS*, Occasional Paper 21, IEA, 1968.

[26] F. G. Pennance, *Housing, Town Planning and the Land Commission,* Hobart Paper 40, IEA, 1967; *Housing Market Analysis and Policy*, Hobart Paper 48, 1969; and *Choice in Housing*, IEA Research Report, 1968; also John Carmichael, *Vacant Possession,* Hobart Paper 28, 1964.

access to employment,[27] the provision of public libraries,[28] and public protection and penal policy.[29]

THE CASE FOR SUBSIDIES

In their enthusiasm for charges IEA authors have a common tendency to underplay the potential importance of different kinds of theoretically valid subsidies which can sometimes cover the whole cost of a service and so make pricing for financial reasons redundant. The most relevant subsidies have three distinct purposes: to promote efficiency in the allocation of resources; to reflect external benefits; and to contribute towards the redistribution of income in favour of the poor.[30]

The marginal-cost-pricing rule provides the justification for the first type of subsidy. Many economists advocate that the price of a service charged to the consumer should equal its marginal cost so as to promote allocative efficiency throughout the economy. When there are economies of scale in production, however, marginal costs will fall below average costs and consumer charges will raise insufficient revenue to cover total costs, and the deficit will have to be financed by a subsidy. In practice, there are a number of technical, so-called 'second-best' problems associated with marginal-cost-pricing which place constraints on its useful-

[27] Christina Fulop, *Markets for Employment*, Research Monograph 26, IEA, 1971.

[28] A. P. Herbert, *Libraries: Free-for-All?*, Hobart Paper 19, IEA, 1962, reprinted in Harris, *op. cit.*

[29] R. L. Carter, *Theft in the Market*, Hobart Paper 60, IEA, 1974.

[30] Ken Judge, 'An introduction to the economic theory of pricing', in Ken Judge (ed.), *Pricing the Social Services*, Macmillan, 1980, pp. 46-66.

ness,[31] but the important point is that in the right circumstances IEA economists would seem to have little objection to subsidies for this purpose. There is considerable opposition from IEA authors, however, to the use of subsidies-in-kind to pursue the second and third of the objectives outlined above.

The *rationale* behind a subsidy to produce external benefits is that it is required to reflect the difference between private valuation and social or élite-group valuation of the benefits of a service. Such external benefits can manifest themselves in a variety of ways. The provision of adequate treatment for an individual with a contagious or infectious disease like typhoid fever or the common cold, for example, could produce substantial benefits for other citizens by reducing their risk of ill-health. On the other hand, the benefits could be less tangible psychic ones, for example, when some aspect of the social and economic status or condition of one individual affects the satisfactions or discomforts of another. Despite these arguments many IEA writers discount or deny the validity of claims that external benefits flow from most social services. Professor Crew and Dr Young, for example, suggest that:

> '. . . some people feel very strongly that the external benefits of education are important . . . But in the absence of hard evidence on the quantitative significance of externalities . . . their supposed existence can easily be used as an excuse for special pleading by interest-groups seeking a larger share of the taxpayers' money'.[32]

[31] C. V. Brown and P. M. Jackson, *Public Sector Economics*, Martin Robertson, London, 1978, pp. 18-20.

[32] Crew and Young, *op. cit.*, p. 18, note 1.

Similarly, Professor Lees argues that knowledge of the external benefits of health care

> '. . . is in practice so limited as to make them a dubious basis for public policy. Certainly, their existence provides no justification for taking medical services out of the market and supplying them free through public authorities'.[33]

PSYCHIC BENEFITS AND UBIQUITOUS EXTERNALITIES

Some of these arguments have a degree of substance, but even if the social rate of return from social services in the form of tangible economic benefits to the community is limited, there are powerful counter-arguments to consider. One such strongly-held view is that citizens do perceive themselves to receive psychic benefits from many social welfare programmes.[34] If this is true it provides a *rationale* for collective behaviour in support of social welfare programmes, and whether this is described as meddlesome or altruistic is largely a matter of taste. The objection to this view, fully expressed by Arthur Seldon, is that it leads one to the conclusion that:

> '. . . everything we do—from eating and drinking to queueing and waiting—affects everybody else, that nothing we do is personal or private, and therefore every activity should be financed by taxes and directed by government officials'.[35]

[33] Lees, *op. cit.*, p. 44.

[34] David Collard, *Altruism and Economy: A Study in Non-Selfish Economics*, Martin Robertson, London, 1978.

[35] Seldon, *Charge*, *op. cit.*, p. 52.

The fallacy of this statement is that not all externalities are relevant for public policy. The only ones that matter are those for which people are willing to pay. Which services generate these external benefits sufficiently to justify public subsidies, of course, is always a matter of dispute. Support for the NHS seems to be widespread whereas hotel accommodation for homeless immigrants is commonly resented. How citizens register their willingness to pay for consumption externalities (which improve their own sense of well-being), therefore, raises a number of interesting questions about the most appropriate mechanisms of social choice. The important point, however, is that there is no reason for believing that political action in support of measures to sustain the flow of these benefits is *necessarily* inferior to activities in the market-place.

A third kind of income maintenance subsidy is often provided specifically to cover the full or partial remission of charges for services, such as free school meals,[36] received by a client who is considered by the social welfare agency to have an income sufficiently low to warrant assistance. The ways in which public agencies assess the remission of charges vary considerably but the most common typically involve detailed means-testing, and a 100 per cent subsidy is often obtainable

[36] Probably the most explicit example of the difference between the external benefit and income maintenance subsidies can be found in the school meals service. All consumers receive a partial subsidy probably designed to reflect the flow of consumption benefits, whereas a sub-group of consumers from low-income families receives an additional subsidy to maintain income in the form of free meals. A sophisticated economic analysis is in Bleddyn Davies, in association with Michael Reddin, *Universality, Selectivity and Effectiveness in Social Policy*, Heinemann, 1978.

only when the consumer has an income at or below supplementary benefit level.

There is a long-standing controversy, however, as to whether the remission of charges, which restricts the subsidy to the consumption of the good or service in question, is the best way of achieving the objectives of income distribution.[37] IEA economists, for example, argue that unrestricted cash transfers usually produce higher levels of welfare or utility for individual consumers than do price subsidies tied to specified services. Moreover, it is generally accepted in the economic literature that this belief is valid, but it does not necessarily follow that restricted transfers are inappropriate instruments of policy. This is because in determining which policy to adopt one needs to take into account the preferences of the provider of the subsidy, or donor, as well as that of the recipient or donee.[38] If the donor gains some satisfaction or utility from the consumption by the recipient of a particular social service, then it will maximise the donor's welfare to insist upon subsidies in the form of specific services rather than cash payments which might be spent on something else.

TEST BY EXPERIMENT

Even after the various subsidies mentioned above have been taken into account it is probable that there might still be arguments in favour of charges. On the one hand, they might be necessary to cover the residual cost of a service after the deduction of subsidies. On the other

[37] Keith Hartley, *Problems of Economic Policy*, Allen and Unwin, 1977, pp. 142-5.

[38] Lester C. Thurow, 'Government Expenditure: Cash or In-Kind Aid?', *Philosophy and Public Affairs*, Vol. 5, Part 4 (1976).

hand, when subsidies total 100 per cent of the cost, it might be thought desirable to use quasi-prices by distributing, say, education or health vouchers to encourage consumer choice. In either case, however, there are at least two further objections to pricing.

First, the use of charges is no more a costless activity than administrative rationing systems and so the size and importance of often complex transaction costs must be taken into account. Although it is usually conveniently ignored, some IEA authors have recognised this argument. Professor Armen Alchian, for example, suggests that some goods and services 'are not priced because the cost of transaction *via* the market is higher'.[39] If we adopt this approach and take into account the various political and social costs, it requires no great leap of imagination to recognise that this argument might be applicable to the use of charges or vouchers in the social services. Almost certainly the transaction costs would be considerable, but we must be careful not to fall into the trap of automatically assuming that they would exceed the benefits of pricing. In the absence of experimental action programmes the balance of costs and benefits cannot be determined.

Another objection to prices is that there are circumstances in which they are not appropriate instruments of policy, when the relevance of consumer sovereignty itself is called into question. Two of the most common arguments are either that the responsibility for choice is not clearly delineated or that individuals are blinded by social and economic forces beyond their control. Is the relevant consumer of compulsory schooling the

[39] Armen A. Alchian, *Pricing and Society*, Occasional Paper 17, IEA, 1969, p. 9.

pupil, his parents or the state? Or is it true, as some economists assert, that individual preferences are not a reliable guide to resource allocation because consumer choices are manipulated by the needs of capitalist production? Professor J. K. Galbraith, for example, argues that producers are able to use advertising and marketing campaigns to alter the perceived wants of individuals.[40]

IEA EMPHASIS ON CONSUMER PREFERENCES: ONUS OF EVIDENCE ON CRITICS

Despite these views, and although most IEA publications are too extremely libertarian for my own taste, their insistence on taking full account of consumer preferences wherever possible is probably their most attractive argument. My own conclusion is that when considering this issue we should follow Dr Albert Weale (Lecturer in Politics at the University of York), in believing that

> 'The burden of proof should rest with those who propose to intervene, rather than those who wish to preserve individual liberty'.[41]

At the very least, a critique of the IEA case which would lead to restriction on pricing must answer the following questions:

(a) How much freedom of choice is permissible for clients of social services?

[40] J. K. Galbraith, 'Economics in the Industrial State: Science and Sedative', *American Economic Review,* 60 (1970), Papers and Proceedings.

[41] Albert Weale, 'Paternalism and Social Policy', *Journal of Social Policy*, 7:2 (1978).

(b) What alternative means of participation in the organisation and delivery of these services are available to consumers?

RE-EXAMINE 'PRIVATISATION', SUB-CONTRACTING, CHARGING, VOLUNTARY ACTION

If the Welfare State is to adjust itself successfully to the harsher economic climate of the 1980s, a shift in thinking is essential. One step in the right direction would be the establishment of a new balance within the *mixed economy of welfare* in Britain.[42] What is required is the greater 'privatisation' of both the financing and production of social services. In particular, there is a widely-held view that the quintessential sickness of government is its inability to provide services efficiently, and that, although it undoubtedly has important responsibilities for the planning and co-ordination of social policy, the state should sub-contract service delivery to private agencies. If a more rational mixed economy of welfare is to be established, the rôles of consumer charges, purchase-of-service contracting, and voluntary and community groups in the provision of collective social services require fresh examination.

It is in this kind of context that the public choice and pricing theories disseminated by the IEA might make an even more significant contribution to the development of new directions in social policy in its next 25 years. But if it is to win new adherents to its ideas it must avoid the appearance of crude anti-statism. In a modern society there will always be some citizens who wish to pursue collective objectives through political

[42] Ken Judge, 'Is there a "crisis" in the welfare state?', *International Journal of Social Economics*, 1981 (forthcoming).

action. It seems reasonable to assume, therefore, that the state will continue to have a part to play in the co-ordination, financing and planning of social services, even if its service delivery rôle is diminished.

What the IEA should be doing in the future is to promote and evaluate experimental developments designed to test the effectiveness of the various instruments available to public agencies in their relationships with private and voluntary providers (such as incentive reimbursement schemes, consumer charges and vouchers, purchase of servicing contracts and quality control systems) which channel demand for, and regulate the supply of, social services in pursuit of the goals of a more pluralist mixed economy of welfare.

Chapter VIII

INTELLECTUAL INFLUENCES IN BRITAIN: PAST AND PRESENT

Ian Bradley

The Author

IAN BRADLEY was born in 1950 and educated at Tonbridge School and New College, Oxford, where he gained a First-Class degree in Modern History and a Doctorate of Philosophy. He is at present a journalist for *The Times* specialising in political and social features. He is the author of four books on Victorian history, including *The Optimists: Themes and Personalities in Victorian Liberalism* (1980), and his latest work is *The English Middle Class* (forthcoming).

Intellectual Influences in Britain: Past and Present

> 'Practical men, who believe themselves to be quite exempt from any intellectual influences, are usually the slaves of some defunct economist. Madmen in authority, who hear voices in the air, are distilling their frenzy from some academic scribbler of a few years back.'
>
> J. M. KEYNES, *The General Theory* (1936), p. 383.

Keynes's famous dictum gives an important, if rather delayed, rôle to economists and other intellectual theoreticians in the formation of practical policy. Contemporary British experience would seem to bear out his observation. Long after they are thought by many to have outlived their usefulness and relevance, it is the ideas of Keynes himself and of Beveridge which still provide the basic assumptions and pre-suppositions for many politicians in government and officials in administration. Only now, 25 years after its foundation, are the very different ideas associated with the Institute of Economic Affairs beginning to achieve anything like the same acceptance in the corridors of Whitehall and Westminster.

LINKS BETWEEN THINKERS AND DOERS

The truth is that in this country the chains that link thinkers and doers in the worlds of politics, economics and public administration are peculiarly weak. Almost uniquely among Western democracies, Britain lacks a system and tradition of free interchange between academia, business, Parliament and administration. We can accommodate Professor Ralf Dahrendorf as an academic, even as an academic administrator running the London School of Economics, but it is impossible to conceive of us accepting him—or a figure of comparable standing born in Britain, like his native West Germany did—as a politician, let alone as a higher civil servant.

Admittedly, British elder statesmen and retired permanent secretaries occasionally become heads of Oxford colleges or go off to run banks and finance houses, and distinguished and normally ageing academics are sometimes given a seat in the House of Lords. Yet this is hardly a substitute for the vigorous interchange between universities, private corporations and public administration that goes on at a rather more youthful and active level, for example, in the United States.

'THINK-TANK' PRESSURE-GROUPS

If Britain lacks this particular mechanism for linking thinkers with doers in economic and political life, it does possess a powerful alternative mechanism in its strong tradition of independent 'think-tanks', seeking both to bring about specific changes in society and to effect a more general change in the prevailing intellectual climate.

Historically, there can be no doubt about the achievements and the effectiveness of those intellectual pressure-groups with specific and defined aims easily translated into legislative action. The abolition of the slave trade and later of slavery from the British Empire, the repeal of the Corn Laws, and the introduction of legislation to regulate the hours and conditions of workers in factories and mines—all these are well-known and well-documented examples of significant reforms brought about largely because of the activity and pressure of lobby groups working from outside to influence legislators at Westminster.

There are numerous more recent examples of equally successful campaigns by pressure-groups leading to major legislative change. The 1967 Abortion Act was introduced into Parliament by Mr David Steel, MP, largely on the basis of the demands being made by the Abortion Law Reform Association. Significantly, the Association was also largely responsible for the drafting of the Act. Even more recently, the last (Labour) Government's introduction of child benefit allowances was almost entirely the result of a successful lobbying campaign by the Child Poverty Action Group.

The impact and influence of pressure-groups like the Institute of Economic Affairs, which seek not so much to campaign for specific changes in legislation or policy, but rather by research and re-education to change the intellectual climate among legislators and administrators, is obviously more difficult to assess. As Keynes's dictum suggests, practical men are notoriously reluctant to admit the influence of intellectual currents. It is nonetheless possible to trace a distinct pedigree of philosophic pressure-groups in Britain over the last 200 years and to make at least some assessment of their success and influence.

THE PHILOSOPHIC RADICALS: THE INFLUENCE OF BENTHAMISM

The Benthamites, or Philosophic Radicals, were perhaps the first pressure-group which sought to change the whole intellectual climate of economic action and policy-making in Britain, and, as such, they are perhaps the original progenitors of the Institute of Economic Affairs. Their leading members flitted in and out of politics and kept in close contact with men of action as well as other men of ideas. Through the Bowood Circle (named after the Wiltshire home of Lord Shelburne), they had a major influence on Shelburne and played a large part in inspiring the movement for economical reform in government for which his Premiership is remembered. Bentham himself managed to leave his mark on a surprisingly wide range of British institutions, not least the prison system, where the adoption of his Panopticon principles[1] had a profound effect on 19th-century penal policy.

The general impact and influence of Benthamism on the state of mind of legislators and policy-makers in the 19th century is more difficult to establish. Few historians now accept A. V. Dicey's bold assertion (in his 'Lectures on the Relations Between Law and Public Opinion in England during the Nineteenth Century' published in 1905) that Benthamism was the dominant influence behind most of the legislation passed in Britain between 1825 and 1870. Indeed, there is now a

[1] The Panopticon was a prison with all the rooms constructed concentrically around a central observation chamber. The principle was put into practice in the building of Pentonville Prison.

vigorous historical debate, and one that is highly pertinent to the impact of IEA thinking on policy, about how far the actions of Victorian governments and legislators were inspired by essentially intellectual currents—whether Benthamite utilitarianism or evangelical Tory paternalism—and how far they were simply the pragmatic response to specific abuses and problems.

Certainly, it is very doubtful if the abstract principle that is perhaps most often (and most erroneously) attributed to Bentham, the doctrine of *laissez-faire*, ever seriously informed 19th-century policy-making. In Britain the classical liberalism propounded by Adam Smith and other economists at the end of the 18th century never really moved out of the realms of high theory. It was certainly never the sustaining ideology of Gladstone's Liberal Party. Victorians who did adhere to an extreme *laissez-faire* position ploughed lonely furrows well away from the centres of political and economic action, like the philosopher Herbert Spencer and the High Court judge Baron Bramwell who delivered lofty judgements asserting individual freedom in its purest and most doctrinaire form.

Where Bentham and his disciples made their more lasting contribution to the intellectual climate of decision-making and policy-forming was in their overwhelming optimism about the possibilities and the likely results of institutional reform and their whole conception of democracy as the rational pursuit of rational ends. The spirit of Victorian liberalism, fundamentally committed to the principle of extending democratic control of government in all its aspects, and fundamentally hopeful about the results, owes much to these Benthamite nostrums.

THE MANCHESTER SCHOOL: IDEOLOGY AND BUSINESS PRACTICALITY

Of even more direct influence on the minds of Victorian Liberals were the ideas of the second great intellectual pressure-group in British history, the Manchester School of economists. Even more than the Philosophic Radicals, the Manchester economists drew their strength from their strong roots in the severely practical business of manufacturing, commerce and politics. They achieved a significant practical victory with the repeal of the Corn Laws in 1846. They had their own group in Parliament, centred around Cobden and Bright and dubbed by Disraeli 'the Manchester Party'. They had important and close links with the other pressure-groups of the 1840s and 1850s that together came to form the nucleus of the Liberal Party.

The ideas which the Manchester School implanted at the heart of the philosophy of the Victorian Liberal Party were simple. They are best encompassed in the famous rallying-cry of 'Peace, Retrenchment and Reform' with the addition of the rock-solid commitment to free trade which has remained, tenuously, a cardinal principle of Liberal doctrine to this day. Of course, it was not only their advocacy by the Manchester economists which made these the principles which informed Liberal government and legislation. They were reinforced by the more practical demands of manufacturers, merchants and administrators. Nonetheless, the ideological input was important.

There are, in practice, good grounds for suggesting that the heyday of Victorian liberalism, the period between the first Reform Act of 1832 and the third of 1885, was uniquely a time in British politics when

Keynes's dictum did not apply and when legislators and administrators were not afraid of intellectualism and ideology. During that half-century the worlds of academia, politics, business, administration and higher journalism did coalesce and overlap to a larger extent than either before or since.

They met in the pages of the great quarterly reviews, in the clubs of Pall Mall and St. James's, and, above all, in such versatile personalities as Gladstone, with his ability to turn from translating Homer or writing a commentary on the Scriptures to composing a budget speech; John Stuart Mill, philosopher, logician and supreme Liberal propagandist and campaigner; Lord Acton, Catholic polemicist and historian of liberty; and John Morley, rationalist, biographer of the heroes of the Enlightenment, journalist and statesman.

These men let their classical philosophy, their Christian scholarship, their rigorous logic and their historical perspectives inform their legislation and their administrative decisions. They were products of an age when politics was not yet a full-time occupation, specialisation had not yet begun to paralyse the academic world, and it was still possible for a man to dabble, and even to excel, in many worlds without being regarded by his peers as either a poor amateur or a dangerous *dilettante*.

VOLUNTARYISM: 1840s-1860s

Even in this favourable *milieu*, however, not all Liberal ideas were transmitted into action. The notion of voluntaryism, first promulgated by Edward Baines and Edward Miall in the 1840s and 1850s, was a case in point, and one with a particular interest for supporters and friends of the IEA.

Voluntaryism is one of the great but neglected doctrines of the Victorian age. Contemporary enthusiasts for such diverse causes as the education voucher, private medicine, workers' co-operatives and 'alternative' communities would all find many of their arguments anticipated in the writing of Baines, the editor of the *Leeds Mercury*, and Miall, a Congregational minister. Both men were first drawn to voluntaryism through their Nonconformist belief that gathered congregations supporting ministers through their own voluntary contributions were closer to the spirit of the Gospel than was the established church supported out of endowments and compulsory church rates.

They developed their views more fully in the vigorous campaign they both waged against the involvement of the state in the funding and provision of schools. They argued on moral, political and social grounds that education was something that could and should be provided voluntarily by parents and not forced on them compulsorily by the state.

There was always a bias in Liberalism towards voluntaryism. When W. E. Forster, the Minister responsible for education in Gladstone's first government (1868-74), introduced legislation to ensure the universal provision of elementary education, it was on the basis that publicly-funded board schools would only be provided in those areas where existing voluntary schools were inadequate. The Liberal Party as a whole, however, never adopted the ultra-voluntaryist position of Baines and Miall. Indeed, even they had by the late 1860s accepted that government control and government money were necessary to educate the huge number of children being born to factory workers. In education, as in other areas, the Liberals were taking their first step towards intervention and collectivism.

THE EMERGENCE OF COLLECTIVISM 1875-1900

What was it, roughly a hundred years ago, which turned the minds of British legislators and policy-makers in a collectivist direction, and gave them a presumption in favour of state action and interventionism in the economy and society? The question is one which is still the subject of much debate among historians. That there was a fundamental change of mood, however gradual, in the last quarter of the 19th century cannot be denied. Even when it is accepted that *laissez-faire* and pure classical liberalism were never the guiding principles that Dicey thought them, there is no doubt of a new collectivist and interventionist mentality coming in around the 1880s.

It is possible to explain this new mood without relating it to any change in the intellectual climate in which policy-makers and legislators were operating. Contemporaries like Sir William Lecky and Sir Henry Maine saw it as a natural consequence of the Liberals' commitment to democracy. In their view, the admission of the ignorant masses to the franchise in the Reform Acts of 1867 and 1885 had reduced politics to the practice of bribery. Almost worse, it had seriously weakened liberty, since the working classes, unlike their social superiors, favoured regulation and restraint. Popular government based on a universal franchise, Lecky predicted, would lead to

'a weakening of private enterprise and philanthropy; a

lowered sense of individual responsibility; diminished love of freedom; the creation of an array of officials, regulating in all departments the affairs of life; the formation of a state of society in which vast multitudes depend for their subsistence on the bounty of the state'.[2]

It is difficult to feel, however, that intellectual influences were not also at work in turning politicians and administrators in a more collectivist direction. For one thing, the new sciences of sociology and statistics were throwing up a whole series of detailed studies, of which the most famous and significant were perhaps those by Charles Booth, which showed that poverty, disease and ignorance were still widespread in Britain, and which, explicitly and implicitly, argued that only state action on a massive scale could eradicate them.

COLLAPSE OF BENTHAMITE OPTIMISM

Equally if not more important was the collapse of the optimism that Bentham had first established and which had sustained the whole Liberal experiment. T. H. Green, while clinging to his Liberal idealist principles, found himself forced to the conclusion that, given the vote and given political freedom, the mass of humanity were not liberated from misery and self-interest and that they could be so liberated only by the actions of a positive state. Graham Wallas, in his *Human Nature in Politics* (1908), finally debunked the whole intellectualist, idealist, optimistic view of political behaviour which had prevailed since Bentham. He wrote:

'Most of the political opinions of most men are the

[2] W. E. H. Lecky, *Democracy and Liberty*, Longman, 1896, Vol. I, p. 227.

result, not of reasoning tested by experience, but of unconscious or half-conscious inference fixed by habit.'[3]

The corollary of this position was the idea of paternalist government by self-appointed experts who knew better than the ignorant populace what was best for them. That principle, together with the related presupposition that the provision of welfare and the running of the economy are better managed by the state than left to individuals, voluntary groups or the free operation of the market, received its fullest expression in the ideology of the Fabians, that small group suffused with middle-class guilt who have cast such a long, dark shadow over 20th-century Britain.

THE FABIANS

In their approach, their tactics and their overall aim of working to effect a complete change of climate in the outlook of governments and legislators, the Fabians stand in the same tradition as the Benthamites, the Manchester School, and the Institute of Economic Affairs. They worked through a variety of methods: by permeation of the Labour Party, by direct activity in the infant London County Council, and by the normal propagandist tactics of pamphleteering and meetings.

The legacy of the Fabians is difficult to assess. Their concrete achievements—the founding of the London School of Economics and the *New Statesman* and the firm implanting of the idea of a universal and comprehensive system of social welfare—are clear enough. They are also closely paralleled by the achievements of

[3] G. Wallas, *Human Nature in Politics*, Archibald Constable (3rd edn., 1920), p. 25.

the IEA—in the founding of the Independent University College at Buckingham in 1975 and of the *Journal of Economic Affairs* in 1980, and the equally firm implanting of the idea of a free market approach to social welfare from the early 1960s. Yet in their wider mission, to collectivise the British middle classes and in particular the leading Liberal politicians of the day, the Fabians themselves in their early years felt that they had failed, though they could not see what was to come later. By 1914 they had abandoned hope in the likes of Asquith, Haldane and Grey, and had reluctantly come to accept that the best hope for socialism in Britain lay with the emergence of a separate Labour Party with strong trade-union roots.

The Fabian ideal of a society planned and run by civil servants armed with a mass of scientific facts and statistical data may not have taken root immediately but it became an important element in the thinking of policy-makers and administrators, reinforcing the natural tendency of civil servants to see themselves as the experts properly entrusted with the government of a wayward and ignorant populace.

Fabianism was not, of course, the sole influence pushing opinion-formers and policy-makers in a collectivist direction in the first quarter of the 20th century, although it had an undeniably pervasive effect, particularly on the emerging Labour Party where the assumptions of the Webbs somehow gained the upper hand over the very different co-operative and libertarian traditions represented by William Morris and guild socialism.

ACADEMIA: THE NURSERY OF COLLECTIVISM

Another key factor were the universities, the common nursery of all leading politicians and administrators of the period. A full study of the influence that, first, the classics departments, then the economics departments, and most recently the sociology departments of universities have had on the thinking of the British Establishment is still waiting to be written, although Arthur Seldon has made some interesting preliminary observations on this theme in a recent issue of *The Times Higher Education Supplement*.[4]

It could well be, however, that when such a study is written it will conclude that British universities have played as important a rôle in implanting a collectivist view of economics and society in the 20th century as they did, at least according to Thomas Hobbes, in spreading the views of politics and government which led to the English Civil War in the 17th century. First Balliol College, and more recently perhaps Sussex University, may yet prove to have been infinitely more important in producing the distinctive cast of mind of the British ruling classes in the last 75 years than the Fabians.

To test the strength of this hypothesis, it is only necessary to reflect on the importance of Balliol in forming the interventionist views of Asquith and then Beveridge (and how important also for Beveridge was his experience in the university settlement movement as a young graduate working in Toynbee Hall). Hardly less significant was the rôle that Cambridge played in

[4] 'Radical Right versus conservative Left', *The Times Higher Education Supplement*, 25 January 1980.

shaping the thought of Keynes. For the next generation of Labour social democrats—Gaitskell, Crossman, Jay and others—Oxford, and especially New College, was to be if anything an even more formative influence.

The economic and political ideas of Keynes and Beveridge took root so quickly within the legislative and administrative establishment, and were translated so fully into policy and action, because they fitted in with preconceptions and attitudes that were already deeply held. They went largely unchallenged chiefly because they were shared by the dominant sources of intellectual influence, the universities, the press, the independent research institutes and the pressure-groups, and also because the war temporarily removed critics like Robbins and Jewkes who might otherwise have challenged them. Together these institutions determined the national agenda of goals. Full employment, universal social welfare, management of the economy and intervention by the benevolent state were high on the list. Libertarianism, freedom of choice, public economy and the values of the market were low, if indeed they were on the agenda at all.

THE IEA AND THE RULING INTELLECTUAL CONSENSUS

It is not too much to say that the Institute of Economic Affairs, when it was formed around 1956, was the first institution seriously to question this ruling Keynesian, Beveridgeite, Fabian intellectual consensus. For virtually the whole of its first two decades of existence, the influence of the IEA on practical policy-making was negligible. It may, perhaps, have had a negative influence in dissuading politicians from grandiose interventionist and corporatist policies, particularly after its critique of the abortive 1965 National Plan. Just about the only major piece of legislation to follow a Paper published by the IEA, however, was the abolition of resale price maintenance in 1964, and there were long-standing administrative and departmental reasons for that decision. The only other governmental decision which was conceivably influenced by the Institute was the decision by the 1970 Conservative administration to introduce competition into banking and break up the cartel.

In its wider rôle of influencing the climate of political and economic opinion, the Institute also made slow progress in its early years, although leading figures from both the Labour and Conservative parties were showing an interest in its publications and seminars by the middle or late 1960s. What really made this side of its work take off was the dramatic conversion in the mid-1970s of the new guiding spirits of the Conservative Party from the Butskellite consensus and the consequent search for a new ideology radically different from the social democracy that had reigned largely unchallenged for so long. It was this sudden, and uncharacteristic, espousal of ideology by the Conservatives, signalled by the creation of the Centre for Policy Studies by Mrs Thatcher and Sir Keith Joseph in September 1974, and by the circulation two years later by Sir Keith throughout the universities and colleges of a 'bibliography of freedom', which included several IEA publications, that put the principles of free market economics and individualism firmly back on to the political agenda. The writing and speeches of the former Liberal Party leader, Jo Grimond, also showed an increasing commitment to the values of voluntaryism and the disciplining of bureaucracy.

* * *

So the centres of intellectual influence on policy-makers and administrators change and shift. The Institute of Economic Affairs may not be in the same league as the Benthamites, the Manchester School and the Fabians, although legislation already passed by the present Government on transport, on education and health care, on council house sales and local government services suggests that its influence is considerable. But at least it is still on the offensive—and, if Keynes is to be believed, the day when its nostrums are finally accepted by practical men will also be the day when it is defunct.

Chapter IX

THE IEA AND THE FABIANS: COMPARISON AND CONTRAST

Colin Clark
University of Queensland, Australia

The Author

COLIN CLARK was born in 1905 and educated at Winchester and Brasenose College, Oxford. He was Lecturer in Statistics, University of Cambridge, 1931-37; Labour parliamentary candidate in 1929, 1931 and 1935; Visiting Lecturer at the Universities of Melbourne, Sydney and Western Australia, 1937-39. He has been economic consultant to the Governments of Ceylon, India and Pakistan, and Financial Adviser to the Treasury of Queensland. Director of the Institute for Research in Agricultural Economics, University of Oxford, 1953-69. Research Fellow at Monash University, Melbourne, Australia, from 1969 to 1976. Dr Clark is now at the University of Queensland, Australia.

He is the author of numerous works, including *The Conditions of Economic Progress* (1940), and has written or contributed to a number of IEA Papers of which the most recent was *Poverty before Politics* (Hobart Paper 73, 1977).

Dr Clark is a member of the IEA's Advisory Council.

The IEA and the Fabians: Comparison and Contrast

There is much truth in the mordant accusation that most of the Conservative Party are not really interested in the question of what policy the country is pursuing. What they consider important is that they should be in power for the administration (for which they consider themselves supremely qualified) of whatever policies they have inherited from their predecessors.

The present mess of nationalised industries, chaotic social services, swollen national and local bureaucracies, and grossly excessive taxation, which a Conservative Government is now administering, is largely the product —how many people realise this?—of the ideas of the Fabian Society in the past. 'In the long run it is ideas which are dangerous, not vested interests', as Keynes wrote.

THE FABIAN SOCIETY AND ITS ANTITHESIS

The Institute of Economic Affairs might be regarded as the antithetical counterpart of the Fabian Society. Both have sought to achieve results the same way, by the dissemination of books and pamphlets, by influencing political leaders and aspirants.

The IEA also illustrates the principle that 'it is ideas which are dangerous'. But ideas require a long time to take effect. The Fabian Society, while obtaining some following among undergraduates (mainly at Cambridge), made little attempt to influence the academic world. Not that, in those days, there was much academic world to influence. There were then few teachers of economics or politics, and governments and the Press took little notice of them. The IEA has grown up in a different world, with a large-scale academic establishment. There can be little doubt about the IEA's success in influencing academic opinion. Free-market economics is now generally taught, except perhaps by a few of the older teachers. But how much time will be required for this change of ideas to result in political action we do not know.

The Fabians, on the other hand, made much more effort directly to influence practising politicians and policy-forming civil servants (the latter categories count even more now than they did then). This is an example the IEA might follow: so far it has been inclined to wait for politicians and civil servants to make their approaches to it.

It is worth examining the Fabian record in more detail. In the final paragraph (p. 204) some suggestions are made of lessons which can be drawn from it.

The record of the Fabian Society has been much misunderstood, particularly by some ill-informed American writers. But in the seminal period 1900-14 the extent of the Fabian Society's influence can hardly be overstated. Paradoxically, it worked largely by influencing Conservative and Liberal statesmen, particularly Balfour, Churchill and Lloyd George—the Labour Party then was of small account.

In those days the Fabian Society had a membership

of only a few hundred, mostly educated and influential people. A proposal, vigorously advocated by H. G. Wells, to convert the Society to a mass movement campaigning throughout the country was decisively rejected by the Fabian executive, and H. G. Wells left the Society. In any case, Sidney and Beatrice Webb had taken a strong personal dislike to Wells, and regarded him as a political liability.

A FORMER FABIAN REMEMBERS

The following is an account from the inside. I was a member of the Fabian Society from 1931 to 1945, and had many long conversations with Sidney and Beatrice Webb.

A strange fact to be taken into account is that the Fabian Society began in 1883 as a religious movement under the title 'The Fellowship of the New Life'. There were many vague ideas of new religions in circulation at that time. Some Fabians followed the strange Indian cult of Theosophy, and practised vegetarianism.

But this phase did not last long. The early Fabians, led by Bernard Shaw and by Beatrice and Sidney Webb, soon decided that what most needed reforming were not mankind's beliefs and morals, but its political and economic institutions.

From the 1860s onward, Marxian doctrine was being preached throughout Europe. The Fabian Society categorically rejected Marxism. This rejection was one of the principal sources of its influence.

Sidney Webb, in 1923, coined the conveniently ambiguous phrase 'the inevitability of gradualness'. To the trade union and party zealots this indicated that change would have to be gradual and not revolutionary; but, at the same time, it indicated that gradual changes were inevitably in the end going to obtain their object. How right he was, unfortunately.

FROM FABIANISM TO TOTALITARIANISM

The Fabian Society rejected all forms of totalitarianism —until the turning point came with the Webbs' visit to Soviet Russia in 1935, when it suddenly became apparent that totalitarianism was the logical development of a Fabian organisation of society.

(This critical visit by the Webbs was preceded by some clowning on a visit to Russia by Bernard Shaw in 1931, in the middle of a famine, which he failed to recognise.)

An important influence in the late 19th century was that of William Morris, a great artist and poet, and designer of a Utopia. William Morris's politics grew, somewhat incongruously, out of his fervent protests (fully justified) against the ugliness of Victorian London, and the contemporary tastelessness of the decorative arts. But readers of his attractive Utopian book, *News from Nowhere*, will see that not only did he emphasise its charms by depicting it in perfect June weather, but also that he projected a totally anarchist (if that were possible) society with no government, no permanent marriage, no regular education, no laws, and no markets, but with men and women all working voluntarily to produce what was needed. Fabians, like many of their contemporaries, were much influenced by Morris's aesthetic ideas.

Society, the Fabians considered, needed regulation and discipline. In their travels the Webbs had visited Japan. This, Beatrice explained to me, was a model of a well disciplined country, in striking contrast to China. (Australia also came in for an unfavourable mention.)

IGNORANCE OF ECONOMICS . . .

But the astonishing thing about the Fabian leaders is that, with few exceptions, they had no knowledge of, or interest in, economics. The Webbs engaged in a long and fruitless denunciation of Marshall, trying to disprove the idea that wages depended on the marginal productivity of labour.

Another extraordinary example is to be found in an entry in Beatrice Webb's diary written in 1927. Referring to the moderate level of unemployment then prevailing (about 5 per cent of the labour force), she attributed it to over-population. Unemployment would not be reduced, she went on to say, until population fell.

. . . AND NAIVE ADVOCACY OF CONTROL BY PUBLIC ADMINISTRATION

The intellectual background of the Fabian leaders, in almost every case, was that of public administration, or historical studies thereof. Public administration is an important subject in itself, and some of the Fabian proposals for reforms in it were desirable. But transferring this concept to advocacy of the whole of economic life being regulated by public administrators is breathtaking in its naïvety.

Business men, it appeared to the Fabians, were less educated and less humane than civil servants; and so what was necessary was the transference of the administration of all business to public officials. It simply did not occur to them that there was an allocation problem, how each enterprise was to obtain the productive resources it required, under constantly changing conditions.

Precisely the same blindness was shown by Lenin. The Russian economy, he said, could easily be regulated by 'a cook' (apparently a derogatory term in Russia). The result, after the Revolution of 1917, and the universal introduction of regulated in place of market transactions, was chaos and famine on an appalling scale. Lenin, in 1921, had to retreat to what was largely a market economy, which lasted until Stalin overthrew it afresh in 1929 (with the result which again included a famine).

Composed almost entirely of educated men and women, the association of the Fabian Society with trade unions, in its early days, was somewhat distant. But then political realism set in. By 1918, when the Labour Party was in sight of becoming the official Opposition, and soon afterwards forming the first Labour Government, Sidney Webb was the main architect of the constitution of the Labour Party, which gives the trade unions a heavily predominating voice in the Party Conference. At the same time the Webbs were firmly opposed to the General Strike of 1926, which certainly did no good to trade unionism.

NATIONALLY REGULATED ECONOMY IN AN OPEN WORLD MARKET

An astonishing paradox was that the strictly nationalised and regulated internal economy was to be open to international free trade. This can perhaps be explained by the practical necessity of maintaining a political alliance with the Liberal Party, which made free trade the principal political issue of those days. This state of affairs lasted until 1931, when the force of world depression caused both Liberal and Labour parties to relapse into protectionism, an attitude which most of them have retained to this day.

The Fabian attitude to foreign affairs was in alliance, not merely with the Liberals, but with the Liberal Imperialists. Shaw, the Webbs and Wells supported the South African War (Boer War) of 1899-1902, an unjust war if ever there was one. This was also true, although they were less demonstrative of their support, of the 1914-18 First World War. Their attitude was in contrast to that of Ramsay Macdonald (who was not a Fabian), one of the very few who faced extreme unpopularity in advocating what, it is now seen, would have been the right policy. The First World War could probably have been settled by negotiation long before it had proceeded to its final stages.

FABIAN PATERNALISM: MUNICIPAL REFORM . . .
Being composed largely of civil servants, professional men, and the like, the attitude of the Fabian Society to ordinary people was very much *de haut en bas*.

> 'We are for the Plebs
> said the Webbs
> the mess they are in
> wants organisin'
> they shall toil, while we spin
> any number of webs.'

This contemporary lampoon accurately conveys the spirit of Fabianism, right down to the aristocratic elision of the final 'g' in 'organising'.

The first efforts of the Fabians were in municipal

administration, which probably did need considerable improvement. 'Natural monopolies'—gas, water and electricity supply, where services cannot economically be competitively duplicated—were undertaken as municipal enterprises (though consideration might have been given to the American alternative of licensed private monopolies with supervised prices). An extended system of secondary education (though probably falling short of that already prevailing in several other countries) was introduced, at the beginning of this century, by the Balfour Government, on Fabian advice.

. . . AND DUPLICITY IN SOCIAL WELFARE

But soon the duplicity began. Sympathetic 19th-century school teachers noticed that some children were coming to school hungry. But instead of organising a service for those in real need, the Fabians took the line that it would be much simpler for the school authorities to provide meals for *all* the children. Some people were too poor to buy books and newspapers. So it was irrationally concluded that the municipal authorities should provide free library service for all, including wealthy families, driving private libraries out of business. And so on.

Then came the irremediable muddle of the state and municipal authorities intervening in the housing market. Most of the shortage of housing was caused by rent regulation, introduced in 1915 as a temporary war-time measure, and remaining with us ever since. This divided the housing market between a favoured party paying low regulated rents, and the disfavoured paying exceptionally high rents. The provision of council houses ever since the 1920s may have been designed, in the first instance, for families in real need. But circumstances change; and the policy has been always to leave families in possession, perhaps with a small increase in rent. The final consequence has been that large sums of public money are being used to subsidise the rents of many families who could well afford to pay a full economic rent.

The converse policy, of providing only temporary housing for families in real need, and requiring them to leave when their circumstances improve, has been practised in the United States. This solution does not work either. To use the American euphemism, public housing becomes filled with 'families with problems', until the neighbourhood reaches such a condition that nobody is willing to live there, even at zero rent. You cannot win. Housing is clearly not a suitable subject for action by public authorities.

Beatrice Webb played an active part in the Royal Commission on the Reform of the Poor Law in 1909. It is generally agreed that the old-fashioned workhouse treatment of poverty was harsh and incompetent and many of the 1909 reforms were needed. But still more does the present-day treatment of poverty by public authorities need improvement. It has only very recently been proposed (the original idea coming from Milton Friedman) that poverty should not be treated piecemeal, but by guaranteeing a minimum income to families in need which they would then spend at their own discretion, not at that of public authorities.

BUREAUCRATIC *v.* GUILD SOCIALISM

While the Fabian Society had, in the field of practical politics, a temporary alliance with the Liberal Party, in the intellectual field it enjoyed some support from Christian social reformers, particularly Chesterton, Tawney and Slessor. But soon there arose a deep division. Led by G. D. H. Cole, a number of younger Fabians viewed with alarm the prospect of a rigidly bureaucratic society towards which Fabian policy was tending. Allied to a few perspicacious trade union leaders, they came to advocate what was called 'Guild Socialism', whereby each trade was to be self-regulating, instead of being controlled by a centralised bureaucracy. This idea appealed to Tawney and Chesterton, although Belloc took it up more cautiously. It was supposedly based on the concept of guilds as they had existed in medieval society. Chesterton may be excused; but Tawney, as an historian, should have known better. More thorough studies, especially by Henri Pirenne, have shown that the medieval guilds, however they may have originated, in time became powerful local monopolies organising comparatively high incomes for themselves, and leaving out in the cold a class of low-paid day-labourers.

The Guild Socialist movement did not last. A number of its adherents, with increasing detachment from reality, became attracted to 'Social Credit', first preached by Douglas in 1918, which would have provided everything to everybody, without any serious effort.

Cole formally abandoned Guild Socialism in 1929, largely under the influence of Gaitskell—pupil influencing tutor?

FABIAN INFLUENCES ON YOUNG PEOPLE

The Webbs liked to keep contact with the younger generation of political aspirants; in some cases (so

Muggeridge reports) actually to marry them off to spouses considered suitable.

Another channel of influence was Hugh Dalton, a pleasant personality, who was largely influential in bringing Gaitskell to the top at an early age. But in spite of his Cambridge degree and his career as a lecturer at the London School of Economics, Dalton had curiously simple economic ideas. Sir Dennis Robertson found much amusement in pointing out how, as Chancellor of the Exchequer from 1945 to 1947, Dalton quite failed to see the connection between the booming internal economy and the persistent difficulties with the balance of payments. Dalton took no interest in Keynes's ideas, wanting a much more regulated economy.

> 'I want to to be able to say to this industry "you expand" —and to that "you contract" '.

After visiting Russia in 1932, and a conversation with Molotov, however, he began to see the difficulties. He said (though would not let himself be quoted):

> 'They are the most inefficient people in the world. I think that it is a disaster for the idea of economic planning that Russia should have been the country where it was first tried out.'

Another channel of communication with the younger generation was the University Labour Federation. However, contrary to what is widely believed, many of the most prominent academics becoming politicians—Gaitskell, Jay and Crossman, not to mention Harold Wilson—took little or no interest in politics in their undergraduate days.

The University Labour Federation was presided over by Arthur Greenwood, who attained Cabinet rank in the 1929 Labour Government. Greenwood also had academic connections (Pigou once crossly referred to him as 'a second-rate extension lecturer'). A skilled politician, holding a key position in the party organisation, a convivial and delightful personality, Greenwood was a man whose ideas, apart from practical politics, were curiously vague and indefinite.

VACUOUS FOUNDATIONS FOR NATIONALISATION

Though it seems incredible, it was on these vacuous foundations that were based proposals for the nationalisation of all the means of production, distribution and exchange. There was no real reason for it; no demonstration of the purpose or purposes of such nationalisation; simply a habitual extension of bureaucracy into ever-widening fields.

It is true that the idea of carrying out such a policy in practice, apart from the limited nationalisations of the 1945 Attlee Government, gradually faded in the Labour Party, though recently revived by the resurgent Left Wing.

It is also true that the idea of nationalising literally everything came somewhat under question, even in the early days. Dalton used to admit exceptions for certain small enterprises concerning which 'we won't bother'. There was also considerable uncertainty about any attempt to nationalise farming. It is true that Stalin did this in 1929, at the cost of permanently low productivity and several years' chaos, which brought Russia to famine.

By the 1950s the policy had been modified to nationalisation of 'the commanding heights'. This phrase, though this was apparently not known by those, such as Crosland, who used it so freely, originated with Lenin. Lenin retained control over certain heavy industries during the 1921-28 period in which he and his successors temporarily retreated from total nationalisation. Not that a nationalised steel industry makes much difference to the course of economic events in other industries—any more than it does in modern Britain. The supposed importance of steel, in many countries, has become a psychological obsession, with the consequence that the world is now facing an almost universal over-capacity for steel production.

In Professor Peter Wiles's words, the British Labour Party, unaware even of the movement towards market allocation of resources in Eastern Europe, remains in a state of 'muddled and moderate Stalinism'.

LABOUR NOT NATIONALISING IN AUSTRALIA

Let me conclude with a little-known episode in modern history, observation of which did not fail to have a considerable effect on me. Under the Australian Constitution the State Governments have all the residual powers of legislation except on the topics specifically reserved for the Federal Parliament. In 1915 a Labour Government was elected in Queensland, which took the doctrine of nationalisation seriously. Already controlling the railways, it set out to nationalise as many local industrial and commercial ventures as it could—not that there were many, in a predominantly agricultural state. The record of these nationalised enterprises was almost uniformly unsatisfactory, with a considerable amount of plain corruption. Labour lost office in 1929 and the new Government sold off all the nationalised enterprises (except the State Insurance Office, which flourishes to this day, based on a monopoly position in Workers' Compensation).

The Labour Party again gained power in 1932, and held it until 1957. In 1938 I was appointed to the post of Economic Adviser to the Governor of Queensland (together with a number of other functions). I soon found out that there was one issue on which this moderate and long-lived post-1932 Labour Government was absolutely determined, namely, not to attempt to repeat its predecessors' nationalisation programme.

CONCLUSION

Fas est ab hoste doceri, as the Latin proverb has it.[1] The experience of the Fabian Society prompts several suggestions for IEA policy.

(i) Attempt to influence politicians and policy-formers in all parties.
(ii) Do not expect immediate results.
(iii) Do not seek mass membership.
(iv) Avoid extremism and excessively doctrinal positions.
(v) Study carefully the details of public administration.
(vi) Cultivate young political aspirants.

[1] 'It is permissible to learn from the enemy'.

Chapter X

THE IEA AS SEEN FROM THE CIVIL SERVICE

Lord Croham
Head of the Treasury 1968-74,
Head of the Home Civil Service 1974-77

The Author

LORD CROHAM was created a Life Peer in 1978. He has been an Adviser to the Governor of the Bank of England since 1978. He entered the Board of Trade in 1939 and held a variety of appointments until he became Permanent Secretary at the Treasury, 1968-74. He was Head of the Home Civil Service and Permanent Secretary, Civil Service Department, 1974-77.

In 1978 he was appointed Deputy Chairman, British National Oil Corporation; Director of Pilkington Bros. since 1978; President, Institute of Fiscal Studies, 1979.

The IEA as seen from the Civil Service

The IEA has consistently advocated the greatest possible reliance on market forces and the least possible government intervention in the economy. Its stance has, therefore, for most of its existence been opposed to prevailing civil service attitudes in individual departments.

Those attitudes are strongly influenced by the government of the day. Only a tiny proportion of civil servants are directly concerned with policy-making, since by far the greater part are concerned with the implementation and execution of prescribed policy. And, while civil servants who are in policy-making areas are critically examining policy options, they are also working to implement the objectives of their Ministers, drawn from whichever of the two major political parties happens to be in power at the time.

OUTSIDE THE MAINSTREAM

Over the post-war period both parties have been inclined to favour interventionist policies, and the IEA has found far more to attack than to praise in the policies of the day. It has therefore more often than not been seen by Ministers and civil servants as lying outside the mainstream of conventional wisdom and advocating unacceptable policies. But the conventional wisdom or consensus of the 1950s and 1960s has become increasingly questioned in the 1970s and 1980s. The fact that the IEA from its inception was questioning that wisdom has undoubtedly given new thrust and impetus to its views today. Its message still secures more response at the political level than from civil servants, but its publications are now studied far more carefully in Whitehall than they used to be.

Most civil servants concerned with departmental policy read widely. They like to familiarise themselves with those criticisms of their departmental policies which may influence the opinion of the Government or Opposition, and which may therefore become part of the currency of parliamentary debate. But only in rare instances do civil servants consider it worthwhile to study in any depth those proposals which do not look like having significant political backing, although they may derive a certain amount of fun or annoyance from reading about them. As a consequence, propositions to which the leadership of both our two major political parties subscribe tend to create a powerful mental resistance in departments to alternative ideas.

'EXTRAVAGANCE': LITTLE PRACTICAL APPLICATION

Largely for this reason, in the 1950s and early 1960s the attitudes of the IEA were regarded in Whitehall as extravagances and of little practical application. This was not because there was any universal belief either in Whitehall or outside it that 'the gentleman in Whitehall knows best'. Rather it came from two generally held views endorsed by successive governments in those years and still highly influential today.

The first of these was that the economic system was not self-regulating but required deliberate and continuous government intervention to ensure full employment without inflation. The second was that freedom of choice when wealth was unequal produced unacceptable inequities, so that the government intervention by physical controls or in other ways was necessary in order to ensure 'fair shares'.

There have been periods of retreat from government intervention, especially when substantial intervention has been seen to be accompanied by unintended and unwanted consequences. Even so, the British economy still experiences a wider extent of government intervention than what have become the most advanced economies, and whether more or less intervention is desirable remains at the core of a political debate in which a wide spectrum of views are held. The IEA has consistently placed itself on one side of this spectrum, emphasising that the disadvantages of government action will always outweigh the advantages. Civil servants tend to occupy a more central position, accepting the case for a considerable degree of government intervention but being well aware of the problems it creates because they tend to be the instruments through which intervention is effected.

Oddly enough, the conventional wisdom about the economic management of the economy which the IEA was consistently to attack was not as firmly established in Whitehall when the IEA came into existence in the late 1950s as it was to become a few years later. At the time the IEA was created, the approach to economic policy which it attacked and has continued to attack had not yet become the unchallenged doctrine of official

UK economic policy which it was to become for the next 20 years. This approach, which may loosely be described as Keynesian, considered that the regulation or management of the economy (largely by fiscal measures) had to be an essential feature of government activity, with the corollary that the government could choose what level of employment (or unemployment) it wanted, always accepting that high levels of employment might be accompanied by inflation.

These ideas had won increasing support during the war and early post-war years, and were fully accepted by most of the younger administrators and economists in economic departments. Many of the older members of the administrative class in the early 1950s accepted them only with considerable reservation. They tended to cling somewhat precariously to the pre-war attitudes which regarded balanced budgets as the proper objective, were worried about too much government intervention (though not happy about abandoning war-time controls too quickly) and about the risk of inflation if too much money was created. With the retirement of this older generation, doubts about the economic rôle of the state receded somewhat, and the IEA, which in large part resurrected the liberal scepticism of the early 1930s, looked 'old hat'.

NOT PRACTICAL POLITICS

As a middle-ranking civil servant at this time I shared most of the prevailing confidence in economic management and planning. But I had some reservations derived from my personal experience of the rigidities of public administration, seen as a war orphan supported by the Ministry of Pensions. I had then acquired an ingrained dislike of the inflexibility inherent in large-scale public administration; a dislike which has never left me. I had also read economics before the publication of Keynes's *General Theory* and under teachers who had serious doubts about many of the fundamental propositions in that book. Even so, although many of the criticisms advanced by the IEA and its authors about the defects of the accepted economic wisdom of the 1960s evoked some degree of sympathetic response in me, I did not regard their alternative proposals as practical politics and I would not think that there were many of my colleagues who did. One took care to note, however, to what extent their material was of interest to Ministers or Members of Parliament.

IEA AND DEA

I remember in 1965, when I was serving in the newly created Department of Economic Affairs, receiving a letter from Arthur Seldon (a contemporary at the London School of Economics in the later 1930s) pointing out a certain overlap in nomenclature with the Institute of Economic Affairs and inviting me to lunch.

We argued among other things about whether economic planning was necessary, possible or anything other than potentially damaging. I defended government policies, believing as I still do that governments must have a strategy for the public sector, and this cannot be either conceived or applied without regard to the rest of the economy. But I privately had mental reservations about whether whatever emerged as government planning in the 1960s would ever be sufficiently realistic to be practicable, since both political parties seemed committed to indicative planning related to growth targets plucked out of the air.

Ralph Harris and Arthur Seldon regarded most of the forecasting and targetry as nonsense and elaborated their market approach, which was a very far cry from the kinds of policies we were currently discussing in Whitehall. I know they did not convince me that any government I was likely to serve in the next decade was likely to follow their prescriptions. I wondered how long their endeavour would last. It was of course the Department of Economic Affairs which was to prove ephemeral, though its demise was more the result of Ministerial changes than a consequence of its policy stance. British enthusiasm for detailed long-term economic planning did not, however, survive the dropping of the National Economic Plan in 1966: so much so that the terms 'economic plan' and 'planning' were under a cloud in Whitehall for over a decade.

READABLE, STIMULATING, LESS DISMISSABLE: THE NEW ORTHODOXY?

In the years that followed I saw and read a great deal of the IEA's output in the economic field, including a substantial proportion of the *Hobart Papers* and *Paperbacks*. They were always readable and stimulating, and I passed many of them on to colleagues. As the years passed, the belief that the British economy was performing poorly reduced confidence in the conventional wisdom, and made it progressively less easy to dismiss the IEA approach as unworkable or not practical politics. There were signs that a growing belief that the public sector had become too big and over-centralised was leading to more interest in alternative ideas.

The big change came after the inflationary explosion which the UK experienced in 1975 and which led to a destruction of confidence in the general character of the economic strategies hitherto followed by successive governments. When in power both major political parties began to regard a high priority for monetary policy as an essential element in their approach to economic strategy and to be concerned about the size of the Public Sector Borrowing Requirement as a factor in money supply. All this influenced attitudes within Whitehall and increased the willingness to examine alternative ideas on all fronts, though always taking into account the basic priorities of the government of the day.

Very soon the Conservative Party was to reject the economic policies it had hitherto embraced and to seek very actively for ways of drastically reducing the size of the public sector and disengaging government from direct detailed intervention in economic decisions. With a party holding such views in power from 1979, many of the views expressed by the IEA had ceased to be heresies and become the new orthodoxy. Many of its publications became prescribed reading for civil servants. But by this time I had long since ceased to be a civil servant.

CHOICE *v.* SOCIAL INEQUITY

During its 25 years the IEA has gathered together a distinguished list of participants and contributors who have challenged conventional wisdom on a wide range of important economic and social topics. Many of these were outside fields with which I was directly concerned. In the changing climate of attitudes, it was at first easier for them to establish that there was something wrong with existing policies than to convince readers that the policies they recommended should be substituted for them.

Typical examples relate to policies on housing, health and education where there is widespread dissatisfaction with the results of present policies in the United Kingdom. Here rapidly rising costs mean that there will either have to be much more public spending or a major change in the methods of funding these services and a degree of return to greater freedom of choice and personal (family) responsibility, which is what many IEA economists would like to see. In these fields, IEA ideas come up against the prevailing belief that any significant departure from the framework we have known (despite its obvious deficiencies compared with what many other countries are achieving) will produce social inequity. This fear of producing social inequity is deeply ingrained in Whitehall, and so long as it remains so civil servants are likely to be highly suspicious of proposals to reduce the rôle of the state, and this for reasons quite unconnected with public sector employment.

A 'USEFUL' ROLE . . . NOT TO BE IGNORED

I know of no way by which the degree of penetration of ideas into large institutions can be reliably measured, especially institutions like the Civil Service whose own basic approach is fundamentally stable but whose actions are directed from above by the more volatile political element in government. Such penetration of ideas is in any event comparatively slow.

Purely as a personal guess, I would say that the influence of the IEA on the Civil Service has never been great but that it is far more significant than it was. I think that it is likely to continue to grow, though other views proposing even more state intervention are likely to have influence as well, since the destruction of a consensus view almost certainly leads to a divergence of attitudes.

I find it hard to believe that the kind of things the IEA authors stand for will become the accepted wisdom of Whitehall in the near future, or that the IEA would be entirely comfortable if that were to happen. As one who welcomes a questioning attitude to any doctrine, I believe that the IEA has performed a useful rôle in destroying some of the illusions and fallacies which underlay many of our mistakes in the post-war period. I believe that it could have an even more useful rôle to play in future. I still do not accept all its criticisms of other approaches nor consider all its ideas to be practical. But I have always felt better able to form my own views on how to deal with a problem when I have heard what the IEA has to say about it.

Chapter XI

THE IEA AS SEEN FROM INDUSTRY

Eric Sharp

Chairman, Monsanto Limited,
Chairman, Cable and Wireless

The Author

ERIC SHARP is Chairman of Monsanto Limited and Cable & Wireless. He has held directorships with British Nylon Spinners, 1957-64; ICI Fibres, 1964-68; Monsanto Europe, 1969; Polyamide Intermediates from 1975. His non-commercial appointments have included UK Delegate, Coal and Petroleum Committees, OEEC, 1948-50; Vice-Chairman, Electricity Committee, OEEC, 1951-54; Secretary to the Herbert Committee of Inquiry into Electricity Supply Industry, 1955-56; Chairman, Chemical Industry Safety and Health Council, 1977-79; President, Chemical Industries Association, 1979-80; Member, London Electricity Board, 1969-78; Economic Development Committee for Chemical Industry from 1980; Central Electricity Generating Board from 1980.

Mr Sharp was appointed CBE in 1980.

The IEA as seen from Industry

The IEA's constant emphasis on the virtues of the free market economy has generally been welcomed by most sections of industry. It should be recognised, however, that many sectors have differing and sometimes conflicting goals. Consequently my comments should be regarded as reflecting my individual views rather than representing industry as a whole.

To the man in the street, the term 'industry' describes an image of manufacturing, probably in decline and beset by insuperable labour and management inefficiencies. In reality, the term 'industry' applies to small manufacturing as well as large capital-intensive companies; to service as well as mineral resource companies; and to nationalised and private sector companies. Some sectors of industry are flourishing and some are declining or in structural transition. Consequently, whilst many companies would welcome a more competitive environment, there are many which seek government intervention for support and market protection—whether through import controls, fiscal stimulus, or incomes policy.

COSTS OF GOVERNMENT INTERVENTION

The IEA's policy over the last 25 years has been one of consistent demonstration of the benefits derived from the allocation of scarce resources through the operation of competitive market forces in a framework of required laws and institutions. In particular, IEA analyses have focussed on the cost of government intervention, with important conclusions for the direction of the economy and for the rôle and structure of government itself. This approach is invaluable, of course, in determining the optimum allocation of resources, particularly in a closed economy. The dilemma confronting British industry, however, is how to compete in export markets or to ward off import penetration when confronted by overseas competition benefiting from subsidies, whether direct or indirect, open or concealed. This raises the relevance of the 'theory of second best' which recognises that where the conditions for optimality may not be attainable, other solutions have to be found. In other words, we may yet have to find more pragmatic answers to the problems of British industry which may depart from the academic ideal of minimal government intervention.

SECOND-BEST POLICY AND THE PUBLIC SECTOR

The last 15-years have borne witness to the failure of our economy to absorb external shocks and to provide real growth in response to fiscal stimulation and incentives. This failure has been apparent in terms of severe economic dislocation—inflation, unemployment, sporadic balance-of-payments and exchange-rate instability, and declining competitiveness of British industry. The Institute's Papers have advocated monetary restraint based on a real reduction in the public sector.

From industry's point of view the advocacy of such

a policy may have an inherent danger, *viz.* monetary restraint may be applied without the essential reduction in the public sector. The second-best policy as seen by British industry would not be one in which the burden falls disproportionately on the corporate sector. Indeed, misapplied monetary policy may prove to be more damaging than misapplied fiscal policy. The IEA in its recent tract, *Is Monetarism Enough?*,[1] has indeed recognised the dangers of an approach which fails to take into account those obstacles which cannot easily be overcome and which have to be accommodated in any successful macro-economic policy.

GOVERNMENT POLICY AND EFFICIENCY IN INDUSTRY

The Institute in the past has focussed its radical theories on the adverse economic consequences of government intervention. Industry may stand to benefit by a more fundamental examination of the factors that affect it directly. Three such factors can be identified: inefficiencies in the use of labour, in management, and in the return on investment. The central problem with which industry requires assistance is to identify the factors that are amenable to correction and those that are for all practical purposes insuperable.

What, for example, are the economic and industrial consequences of labour immobility? How can impediments be removed? What effect does wage policy have on productivity, i.e. is overtime used to compensate for managerial inefficiency and low average hourly earnings? Is there a correlation between poor labour rela-

[1] IEA Readings 24, 1980.

tions, plant size, location, and new *versus* old plants? What are the consequences of tax structure and marginal tax rates on productivity both on the shop floor and on managements?

If the decline of relative productive efficiency is to be arrested, British industry must seek answers to these and other questions, and here, clearly, IEA authors can make an important contribution. I recognise that some of these questions may be resolved only by the analysis of industrial behaviour. Although such analysis is likely to be unappealing to those used to rigorous statistical or econometric techniques, many of the issues raised above, particularly those relating to labour problems, inevitably involve behavioural factors. Furthermore, similar analysis could indicate whether British companies' internal structure or management style promotes risk aversion or causes the value of research and development, for example, to be under-emphasised. The Institute's approach has implicitly recognised the importance of motivation and attitudes in the application of economic theory to specific issues, and industry would welcome the extension of the IEA's interest into aspects traditionally regarded as the preserve of the sociologist.[2]

MICRO-ECONOMIC MORE IMPORTANT THAN MACRO-ECONOMIC

It has often been repeated that industry has to plan its development on a time-scale longer than that normally encompassed by government. The Parliamentary life of

[2] [The Social Affairs Unit, which will apply sociology to a wide range of activities including industry, was formed in 1980 as an offshoot of the IEA.—ED.]

an administration is, on the average, four years. During that period, industry is affected by annual domestic budgets introduced by Chancellors of the Exchequer as well as by changes in the external environment. The Institute's macro-economic interests are broadly concurrent with those of industry in being concerned with the medium- and long-term conditions for a stable economy.

The experience of the last 15 years has been a record of constant fluctuations in economic, financial and industrial policies that have consequently promoted uncertainty and defensive corporate strategies. Against these fluctuations in government policies, the IEA has correctly identified the overriding importance of micro-economic considerations which have been more relevant to the problems of British industry than the objectives and policies of post-war governments concerned with demand management. Further, the IEA's continual critical examination of the economic consequences of the expansion of central and local government has defined the burden which the private sector has increasingly had to bear. The IEA has played an invaluable rôle in clarifying and evaluating alternative strategies in financing and supplying government services.

In considering the obstacles to growth, it is appropriate to focus on those aspects of investment appraisal affected by government policies. The real rate of return before tax for industrial and commercial companies has declined from 10·3 per cent in 1966 to 8·6 per cent in 1972 and to 4·5 per cent in 1977. Whilst management must bear some responsibility for poor investment decisions, it is clear that a larger share of responsibility must be attributed to government policies which have increased costs, reduced the real value of money return, and fostered uncertainty associated with investment. In contrast, the returns to lenders to the public sectors (i.e. investors in Treasury Bills) have been appreciably higher than returns to investors in industry.

AUTOMATION AND EMPLOYMENT

The Institute's emphasis has constantly been on the freedom for expression of consumer preferences and the related allocation of resources. It has pursued optimality through the operation of the pricing mechanism in a free market economy. A central issue which society will be confronting is the technological impact of automated production on the level of employment. Keynes's *General Theory of Employment, Interest and Money* was developed in the 1930s, assuming under-employment of resources and the capacity of the economy to achieve full employment. The challenge that industry will face is whether the UK economy can be organised to minimise structural unemployment without adversely affecting competitive efficiency. The challenge that the IEA will face is the development of a response consistent with its current approach. It is by no means obvious that government ought not to intervene to alleviate the social consequences of massive structural unemployment or to assist industry in the development of new growth sectors.

COMMON GROUND BETWEEN KEYNES AND THE CLASSICAL SCHOOL

IEA authors have been categorised as the ardent exponents of the austere Classical school of economic thought in contrast to the Keynesian school, which has been identified with the enlargement of the functions of government, particularly in the management of the economy through influence on the propensity to consume and invest. The attraction at the political level of the Keynesian approach is the desire to increase effective demand, especially in the current circumstances of high unemployment, or, as Keynes put it, 'the public scandal of wasted resources'. What is likely to be overlooked in this fundamental economic debate is the common ground between the IEA, the Classical school and Keynes, which also reflects equally the view of industry. This common ground is best expressed in Keynes's own words in his *General Theory*:

> '. . . the result of filling in the gaps in the classical theory is not to dispose of the "Manchester System", but to indicate the nature of the environment which the free play of economic forces requires if it is to realise the full potentialities of production. The central controls necessary to ensure full employment will, of course, involve a large extension of the traditional functions of government. Furthermore, the modern classical theory has itself called attention to various conditions in which the free play of economic forces may need to be curbed or guided. But there will still remain a wide field for the exercise of private initiative and responsibility. Within this field the traditional advantages of individualism will still hold good.
>
> 'Let us stop for a moment to remind ourselves what these advantages are. They are partly advantages of efficiency—the advantages of decentralisation and of the play of self-interest. The advantage to efficiency of the decentralisation of decisions and of individual responsibility is even greater, perhaps, than the nineteenth century supposed; and the reaction against the appeal to self-

interest may have gone too far. But, above all, individualism, if it can be purged of its defects and its abuses, is the best safeguard of personal liberty in the sense that, compared with any other system, it greatly widens the field for the exercise of personal choice. It is also the best safeguard of the variety of life, which emerges precisely from this extended field of personal choice, and the loss of which is the greatest of all the losses of the homogeneous or totalitarian state. For this variety preserves the traditions which embody the most secure and successful choices of former generations; it colours the present with the diversification of its fancy; and, being the handmaid of experiment as well as of tradition and of fancy, it is the most powerful instrument to better the future.'[3]

[3] J. M. Keynes, *The General Theory* . . ., Macmillan, 1936, pp. 379-80.

Chapter XII

THE POWER OF IDEAS OVER POLICY

Norman Gash
Professor Emeritus,
University of St Andrews

The Author

NORMAN GASH was born in 1912 and educated at Reading School and St John's College, Oxford, at which he was a scholar. He has taught history at the Universities of Edinburgh, London, Leeds and Oxford. From 1955 until his retirement in 1980 he was Professor of History at the University of St Andrews, where he was Vice-Principal 1967-71 and Dean of the Faculty of Arts, 1978-80. His main published works are *Politics in the Age of Peel* (1953); *Mr Secretary Peel* (1961); *Reaction and Reconstruction in English Politics, 1832-52* (1966); *The Age of Peel* (1968); *Sir Robert Peel* (1972); *Peel* (1976); *Aristocracy and People: Britain 1815-1865* (1979). For the IEA he wrote an essay, 'The State of the Debate', for the 2nd Edition of *The Long Debate on Poverty* (Readings 9, 1974). He also contributed a chapter on 'The British Party System and the Closed Society', in *The Coming Confrontation* (1978).

The Power of Ideas over Policy

The nature of the IEA has been described often enough, by its spokesmen and also by its critics. Put simply, it is a purveyor of ideas. Its character derives from one central idea; its function is to apply that idea to contemporary society. As an institution it is dedicated (in Lincolnian language) to the proposition that, beyond a certain point, the social and economic intervention of government, however worthily motivated, is self-defeating, and that greater economic and ethical advantage will result from allowing individuals to pursue their own self-motivated activities. The business of the IEA is to apply that idea to an analysis and critique of the collectivist machinery, and, even more importantly, of the collectivist mentality which has grown up in Britain during this century. The 25 years that the IEA has been in business is long enough to justify in a review of its efforts the inclusion of some reflections on the larger problem of ideas in history.

IDEAS INTO ACTION: 'FAVOURING CIRCUMSTANCES'

Ideas, like inventions, need favouring circumstances to achieve historical success. The precocious scientific brains of Albertus Magnus and Roger Bacon were wasted on the Europe of the 13th century. Even the inventive genius of Leonardo da Vinci was doomed to comparative sterility by the limitations of his age. Compare their fate with the dozens of clever engineers and artisans like Watt, Arkwright, Brunel and Stephenson who rose to fame and affluence in the Industrial Revolution. It is the same with ideas. To become historically significant, ideas must influence men's minds and stimulate their actions; and they must do this in such a way as to have a tangible effect on the world of events. Application is everything. The worthy Sir Robert Filmer is now a forgotten man; but his book *Patriarcha, or the Natural Power of Kings,* published in 1680, had a great reputation in its day because it was an effective statement of a theory of government which came naturally to many educated people in 17th-century England. Thomas Hobbes, on the other hand, the most profound and original English political theorist of that period, whose classic work *Leviathan* is still a set text in academic curricula, had no influence in his own time and was simply regarded as a very wicked man.

It is possible, of course, though not especially rewarding, to regard ideas as absolute and philosophy as eternal. In a world of pure scholarship this attitude may be defensible; but such a world is not one which many of us inhabit. Philosophers themselves may spend much of their professional time in such rarefied regions but even they in their ordinary lives are obliged to submit to more mundane considerations. Even so, it is an occupational weakness of intellectuals to attach excessive importance to ideas in the abstract; to judge them, that is to say, by what they are, not by what they do.

The historian employs—or ought to employ—different criteria. He does not concern himself with the truth, the beauty, the subtlety or the symmetry of ideas. His sole test is whether ideas affect events; and he knows that a stupid or a crude doctrine may (often does) have more influence than an elegant or clever doctrine. Many politicians would be out of a living were it not so. Indeed, it is often the case that not until ideas have become coarsened and vulgarised, have become, through much handling, so to speak, sufficiently debased for common use, that they begin to have an effect on events. If ideas do not affect events they are of little historical significance, however much they may interest the intellectuals. This is the difference between the 'history of ideas' and 'ideas in history'. For the historian the first question is not 'Who?' but 'Whom?': not who originated this idea but whom did this idea influence? The next question is 'Why?' Why was this idea effective at this particular time? And the last is 'What'? What was the result of it all?

BETTERING THE HUMAN CONDITION

It is important to make this distinction because there is a natural tendency among educated people to believe that it is enough to enunciate true or good or benevolent ideas for them not only to be accepted but to be acted upon. This is particularly so with those philosophies or programmes which take as their province the betterment of the human condition. The history of human society is littered with well-meaning reformers who optimistically put forward schemes of action which, in Oswald Spengler's mordant phrase,

> 'rest upon the hypothesis that all men are as rich in ideals and as poor in motive as the author is (or thinks he is)'.[1]

In practice, it does not take much observation to conclude that most people, once they emerge from adolescence, tend to shed ideals and, as recompense, acquire motives. It is natural after all to wish to stay alive, to have a roof overhead and food on the table. The pursuit of these reasonable objectives does not always leave much time for idealism. The taste for that comes after the more basic needs are satisfied; and not always then.

This is not to argue that ideas are separate from ordinary life. On the contrary, they are as much a part of human existence as food and shelter. But there is an important distinction between ideas in the head and ideas in action. When ideas, particularly ideas about human conduct, are put into practice, they tend to assume a life of their own, to operate differently from the expectations of their authors, to have unpredictable, sometimes disillusioning, occasionally tragic, results. The combination of abstract ideals and political passions, for example, is peculiarly volatile. In the right circumstances and the wrong hands it can be as lethal as high explosive. Look at the historical (as distinct from the philosophic) consequences of Rousseau's *Contrat Social* or Marx and Engels's *Communist Manifesto*. The perils implicit in abstract ideas when they become part of great political movements were perceived by Edmund Burke two centuries ago: 'In the groves of *their* academy', he wrote of the French

[1] Oswald Spengler, *The Decline of the West*, George Allen & Unwin, 1932.

political intellectuals of his own time, 'at the end of every vista, you see nothing but the gallows.'

IDEAS AND INTERESTS

These are extreme examples; not all political ideas have the properties of dynamite. But the general principle is sound. To be historically important, ideas must not only enter men's minds but shape their actions. They will not do this, however, unless there is a further element present. It is this which makes the difference between the ideas elaborated in the antiseptic pages of the book or pamphlet and what happens when they are removed into the unhygienic real world and put into practice—or attempted to be put into practice.

People must have a motive and an interest in accepting new ideas and allowing them to influence their conduct; and those interests and motives, generally speaking, are to be looked for in contemporary circumstances. The more abstract the ideas, the more room there is, so to speak, for historical improvisation. That is to say, the more they will be coloured by the fortuitous events of their time and the more they are likely therefore to diverge from the intentions of their authors. When ideas are kept within bounds and under control, they are usually practical in character, limited in application, and directed to the immediate and perceived problems of their age.

DISTASTE FOR ABSTRACT IDEAS, TASTE FOR BLOODLESS REVOLUTIONS

One reason perhaps why the course of British politics over the last three centuries has been singularly free from the violent struggles and revolutions that have marked the history of the European mainland is that the British people have on the whole shown a distaste for abstract doctrines. The Civil Wars, regicide and revolutions of the 17th century acted as a kind of timely purge for the body politic. No pitched battle has been fought on English soil since 1685; none anywhere in Britain since 1746; no foreign invasions have taken place in any real sense since the Norman Conquest. These unusual circumstances have created a fundamental sense of security rare among European states; and absence of fear has bred an instinct for moderation.

The British prefer practical programmes for immediate needs rather than a manifesto of abstractions. The 'liberties of Englishmen', the 'freedom of the subject', even the 'rights of trade unions' have meant more than 'the rights of man', the 'victory of the proletariat' or the 'class war'. Whether conscious or unconscious, the avoidance of continental Socialism by the early Labour Movement was a powerful factor in its acceptance by British society—including the middle as well as the working classes. The intellectual roots of the British Left in the 19th and early 20th centuries are to be found in John Stuart Mill, Ruskin, Matthew Arnold, William Morris, Shaw, Wells and the Fabian Society, along with liberal writers like L. T. Hobhouse and J. A. Hobson, rather than in Hegel, Marx, Engels, Lassalle and Lenin. As late as 1927 Ramsay Macdonald could still assert that 'the Labour Party is not Socialist'; and the Fabian slogan of 'the inevitability of gradualness' was a more effective cry, re-assuring to both friends and enemies, than any summons to the barricades. The English, on the whole, like to carry out their revolutions bloodlessly, by due course of law, and over a long period of time. They are none the less revolutions for all that; though this frequently escapes the notice of foreign observers.

The rise of the Labour Party is itself an interesting example of the interaction of ideas and practice. While it is almost certainly true that without the wealth and organisation of the trade union movement it could never have displaced the Liberal Party so rapidly as the second major element in an essentially two-party system, yet it is equally true that this rise to power took place in an intellectual climate of opinion highly favourable to state intervention and collectivist action. Long before the electoral victory at the polling booths was achieved, a significant ideological victory had been won by the sustained campaign that ran with increasing strength from the publication of Henry George's *Progress and Poverty* in 1879 to the prolific Left Book Club of the 1930s.

INTER-WAR COLLECTIVIST SATURATION

Today, when the Left is on the defensive, if not intellectually bankrupt, it is difficult to realise the extent to which the younger generation between the wars grew up in an intellectual atmosphere saturated by socialist and collectivist thought. Equally striking in retrospect was the absence of any coherent body of doctrine raised in opposition to it. From the intellectuals themselves, including many who regarded themselves as conservative, there was little constructive resistance. A generation of Oxford and Cambridge dons, reared on the watered-down Hegelianism of T. H. Green, Bradley and Bosanquet, were in no position to furnish any radical criticism of fashionable trends

—even if they had wished to do so. 'In 1914 orthodoxy [implying academic orthodoxy] means belief in the State, and heresy takes the form of mild excursions into anarchism', wrote Ernest Barker, the Cambridge academic, in 1915, 30 years before the advent of the first Labour Government armed with real political power. Argument alone would never have produced Mr Attlee's government. But what the rise of an electorally powerful Labour Party during the 1930s demonstrated was the importance of ideas and arguments when they are in harmony with other social and political tendencies. Long before 1945 British society was permeated at all levels by collectivist thinking.

IDEAS WORK THROUGH MINORITIES

Certainly motive and interest are needed for ultimate success. Yet in turn a sustained intellectual campaign sharpens motive and enlarges the area of interest. Ideas can act as the solvents of conventional thinking; they can harness prevailing discontents; they can stimulate action. They form the cutting-edge of social and political movements, enabling them to move faster and with more assurance. It is not even necessary for all or even a majority to be converted before ideas can be said to succeed. It is enough if a convinced minority in a position of power can be moved to action. The mass of people, especially if they are restless under the existing system, can easily be brought to assent to a coherent and confidently proclaimed programme of change.

Most conscious political efforts are carried out by minorities. The art of the propagandist (using that term in a neutral sense) is to know the particular élite which it is desirable to convert. The Jesuits discovered this secret in the 16th century. In the end, the new ideas in a cruder and more generalised form will be accepted by the majority. But this belated popularity often comes only after the decisive action has already been taken.

FREE TRADE: 1783 TO 1865—PARALLELS WITH 1980s?

An interesting case-book example of a revolution carried out by an intellectual minority is provided by the Free Trade revolution in British government policy between 1783 and 1865. It has many obvious parallels with our own time.

The historical circumstances which provided the motive force were various: the rapid development of British commerce and manufacture in the early Industrial Revolution; the increasing diversification of British society, in particular the growth of the educated and wealthy middle classes; the apparent inefficiency of government demonstrated by the disastrous American War (1776-1783); the financial strain of administering and protecting a large and constantly expanding colonial empire; the growth of the National Debt which alone bridged the widening gap between expenditure and revenue; the obsolescence of the structure of the state, which had remained largely unaltered since the upheavals of the 17th century; the abuse of government patronage for private and party purposes which aristocratic politics had erected into a technique of government; and, finally, the notorious absurdities and anomalies of the electoral system.

THE INTELLECTUAL ASSAULT

The intellectual attack on this vast interlocking structure (what Cobbett a generation later was to call 'The Thing') was initiated by a group of able theorists headed by David Hume, Adam Smith and Jeremy Bentham. The symbolic starting-point is conveniently found in the year 1776 which saw the publication of Smith's *Wealth of Nations*, Bentham's *Fragment on Government* and the American *Declaration of Independence*. Even today the American constitution bears the signs of having been born in the intellectual atmosphere of a libertarian revolution. Once launched, the intellectual campaign was carried on by a host of lesser writers for another two generations until it subsided into orthodoxy and complacency.

As far as politics and economics were concerned, the main features are easily distinguished. Negatively it was an attack on the complications and waste caused by extensive, unnecessary and arbitrary intervention by the state in the ordinary affairs of life, the result of two centuries or more of unco-ordinated, haphazard legislation. On the positive side, it was inspired by the rationalist philosophy of the 18th century which taught (in reaction against the theological approach of previous centuries) that there was an innate commonsense in human beings when freed from sinister interests or state corruption; that there was therefore an intrinsic tendency towards order and stability in human society, an equilibrium to which it would always instinctively swing provided there was no artificial pressure forcing it off-balance. It was a philosophy consequently of both liberty and individualism, the one unattainable without the other.

A REVOLUTION INSPIRED FROM THE TOP

The striking aspect of the transition from the over-regulated, protectionist economy of the 18th century to the liberal free-trade economy of the mid-19th century is that it was inspired as well as directed from above. Some of the earliest disciples of Adam Smith were leading politicians, including no less than four of George III's Prime Ministers—Lord North, Lord Shelburne, Lord Grenville and the younger Pitt. Free-trade ideas, in other words, entered the citadel of power before they influenced the outworks. To this list of early free-traders can be added Lord Liverpool, the last Prime Minister to hold his office continuously during five successive parliaments (1812-27). He read Hume when an undergraduate at Oxford, was made to study political economy by his ambitious father (the first President of the newly-formed Board of Trade), and was proud to acknowledge himself in later life a follower of Adam Smith, whom he once described to the House of Lords as 'perhaps the greatest philosopher that ever existed'.

The work of dismantling the ponderous machinery of the 18th-century mercantilist state was spread over two generations. There was a prologue under the younger Pitt before the French Wars began in 1793 and an epilogue under Gladstone when Chancellor of the Exchequer between 1852 and 1865. The decisive effort, however, was made in two spells of intensive activity: under Liverpool, Wallace and Huskisson in the 1820s, and under Peel in the 1840s. In those two crucial periods, separated by a decade of Whig rule (1830-41) which saw much constitutional but little economic reform, the greater part of the enormous mass of restrictive legislation governing the movement of imports and exports was removed and the basis of the national revenue remodelled. In both phases it was significant that the government was acting under the immediate pressure of events. Though the form of their actions may have been predetermined by their existing set of ideas, the need for action grew out of existing circumstances. For Liverpool these were provided by the post-war depression, unemployment, and the financial insolvency of the 1816-19 years; for Peel by the industrial depression of 1837-42, the prolonged deficiencies in the revenue during that period, and the social disorder of the Age of Chartism.

RESISTANCE TO REFORM

Even so, the Free Trade revolution in government policy was achieved not so much in response to public demand as in the face of doubtful sympathies and sectional opposition. The mercantile and industrial interests which stood to gain most from the new policy were slow to appreciate what was being done for them. The famous 1820 Free Trade petition of the London merchants, for example, which is often quoted as evidence to the contrary, was a misleading phenomenon. It was prepared by a theoretical economist, Thomas Tooke, and met with little response from the practical men in the City until it was taken up by the influential banker, Henry Thornton, and given active encouragement by the Prime Minister, Lord Liverpool. Though Free Trade was by this date the approved economic doctrine of the intellectuals, including many politicians, few industrial or mercantile interests were anxious to expose themselves voluntarily to the untempered winds of competition. The loosening of the tariff system and the dismantling of the Navigation Acts met with determined resistance from the trades and industries most affected; as did the early efforts by the Government to reduce the high protection for corn imposed at the close of the Napoleonic Wars.

Abstract acceptance of the principle of the new liberal economic policy was combined with a human reluctance to see it applied too drastically in any specific instance. Most interested parties were prompt with reasons why they constituted a case for special exemption from a principle which doubtless was valid for others. It was the same with Peel's great budget of 1842 which lowered tariffs on the majority of dutiable goods entering the country as well as sharply reducing the already modified scale of duties imposed by the Corn Law of 1828. All the Prime Minister's firmness was needed to resist backstairs political pressure and private lobbying. 'Concessions to any demand which we do not feel *bona-fide* a good one', he wrote to his President of the Board of Trade, 'will involve ourselves in greater difficulties than direct opposition publicly offered.'

INCOME TAX REFORM

The importance of ideas and leadership in the Free Trade Revolution can be illustrated most effectively perhaps by two episodes: the resumption of the income tax and the repeal of the Corn Laws. As far as the first was concerned, financial reform was an indispensable part of any radical free-trade policy. Traditionally, the bulk of the national revenue was expected to come from customs and excise. Unless some substitute tax could be discovered, tariffs could not be lowered beyond a certain point without imperilling the financial solvency of the state—as the Whigs had discovered in the 1830s. By that time most experts were agreed that the only solution was to revive the income tax. This was a wartime emergency tax, new in theory and hated in practice, which had been introduced in 1799 and terminated in 1816. The Government had proposed to continue it in peacetime as a means of solving its predictable post-war difficulties. The House of Commons, stiffened by public agitation, obliged the Ministers to abandon it.

It was a loss Liverpool never ceased to deplore. 'No other tax', he once observed, 'was so equal or so just'. But for politicians and the public it remained an article of faith that such a tax, simultaneously inquisitorial and inescapable, would never be accepted by the British people in time of peace. The pundits, however, continued to regard it as the only way to extricate government from its recurrent financial embarrassment. There was talk in the privacy of the cabinet of reviving the tax in 1829; but nothing was done until 1842, when it formed part of Peel's revolutionary budget of that year. Even members of his own cabinet were fearful of the political consequences when it was mooted in ministerial circles; and the parliamentary opposition disbelieved up to the end that the Prime Minister would have the courage—or foolhardiness—to propose it. Ironically, in view of that controversy, no subsequent Chancellor of the Exchequer has ever felt able to do without it.

CORN LAW REPEAL AND ROBERT PEEL

The Corn Laws provide an example of a different sort. The myth still lingers that it was the propaganda of

Cobden, Bright and the Anti-Corn Law League which in 1846 finally persuaded the British people (and Peel) that the Corn Laws must be abolished. In fact the demand for their repeal had been a feature of radical agitation ever since 1815. It was because the idea of repeal was so familiar, not because it was so novel, that the League was able to make such rapid headway. The radical aristocrat Villiers had since 1837 staged annual debates in the House of Commons on the question which revealed the growing parliamentary support for review if not outright repeal. The three statutory changes in the law that took place between the original high protective Act of 1815 and repeal in 1846 were in themselves ample evidence of the sensitivity of successive governments to the problem.

The Manchester Anti-Corn Law League of Cobden and Bright was simply the best-known and most active, but not the first nor the only society of its kind. Moreover, what convinced Peel in 1846 was not the arguments of the League with which he had long been familiar but his own fundamental free-trade philosophy, the practical success of his free-trade budgets between 1842 and 1845, and the growing conviction that for political reasons alone the landed interest could not, in isolation from the other great economic interests of the country, retain a highly protected industry in an increasingly free-trade economy.

It was one thing, however, to be persuaded that the Corn Laws were both politically unpopular and practically inefficient. It was a different matter to translate conviction into action when action meant passing legislation through a Parliament dominated by landowners. 'No living soul,' acknowledged one of his parliamentary opponents, 'could have done this but Peel.' He had intended to announce his change of mind over the Corn Laws before the 1847 general election. It was the failure of the Irish potato crop in 1845 that forced his hand and produced the spectacular decision which broke his party and ended his ministerial career. The League was only one element in a complex political situation.

CREATING OPPORTUNITIES FOR REFORM

Historical circumstances can never repeat themselves, though they may sometimes bear a certain resemblance to each other. The historian, unlike astrologers, fortune-tellers and economists, does not presume to forecast future events. The most he can offer are reflections, suggestive perhaps but inconclusive, on the nature of human affairs.

The relationship between ideas, circumstances and personalities is a subtle one. If ideas shape action, action often modifies, sometimes transforms, ideas. Circumstances may provide opportunities; but opportunities can frequently be created. The task of the theorist is to formulate ideas; that of the politician is to attempt to translate them into action. The most hazardous part of that attempt is to judge correctly when circumstances are ripe for action. A politician may be no more than a dealer in obvious possibilities—an agent of the commonplace. A statesman is one who sees possibilities where lesser men see only impossibilities. Even so, without ideas to give shape and direction to his statesmanship, he is unlikely to achieve much. The aimless, the accidental and the unforeseen play a large enough part in human affairs, without needlessly relying on them for inspiration or advantage. Even politics cannot safely dispense with the intellectual process.

Certainly no study of British political history over the last two or three centuries can sensibly ignore the rôle of ideas. The influence of Locke and the Whig rationalists of the 18th century, of Adam Smith and Jeremy Bentham in the late 18th and 19th centuries, of the collectivists and socialist writers since 1880, were in their day of incalculable significance in preparing, justifying and shaping larger historical changes. The intellectual reaction against collectivism has found expression in a variety of ways over a long period; from such half-forgotten books as W. H. Mallock's *Critical Examination of Socialism* (1908) and Belloc's *Servile State* (1912) through Lord Hewart's *New Despotism* (1929) to Milton Friedman and F. A. Hayek in our own time. But it would be difficult to find any other single source that has contributed so continuously, ably and comprehensively as the IEA to the intellectual undermining of the collectivist state. The anti-collectivist revolution in thought cannot boast (in this country at least) an Adam Smith or a Jeremy Bentham, any classic like the *Wealth of Nations* or the *Contrat Social.* Yet at least it can be said that a liberal market institution, by attracting to itself innumerable writers, has become the uncrowned academy of the new thinking.

End-piece

HOW IT ALL BEGAN—PERSONAL RECOLLECTIONS

John B. Wood

The IEA might so easily not have happened. But for a few chance meetings some 25 to 35 years ago between a handful of people, then strangers to each other, the act of creation might never have taken place.

Suppose, for instance, that in 1945 Antony Fisher, just de-mobilised from the RAF, and already worried by the way the post-war world was developing, had not read a summary of Professor Hayek's *Road to Serfdom*, and found its warnings so confirmed his own apprehensions that he sought out the author, . . .[1]
—and suppose that Professor Hayek had failed to dissuade him from, as he then contemplated, going into politics, urging him instead to set up a research organisation to influence intellectual economic opinion, . . .
—and suppose further that in 1949 Ralph Harris had not accepted a speaking invitation in East Grinstead at which Antony Fisher happened to be in the audience,

[1] For further detail, Antony Fisher, *Must History Repeat Itself?*, Churchill Press, 1974, p. 103 *et seq.*

and, recognising a fellow spirit, exchanged addresses—though they were not to meet again for five years, by which time Fisher's Buxted Chickens business was fortunately making profits, . . .

—and suppose, lastly, that Arthur Seldon, through his work for the Liberal Party before and after the war, had not known Lord Grantchester, an early member of the IEA's Advisory Council, who put forward his name in 1956 as a possible author of a book on pensions, . . .

—then surely it is not only this book or the 300 IEA titles that would not have been written. But for these chance meetings and acquaintances, it is doubtful whether the prevailing post-war economic orthodoxies would have been challenged so successfully that opinion and policy were eventually to be shifted in quite a different direction. Is it too much to discern here, not for the last time in the IEA's history, the faint silhouette of an invisible hand?

'A HAVEN FOR REFUGEES'

The emergence of the IEA is a good illustration of the social philosophy with which it is now identified, namely, that most creative developments in society result from harnessing the spontaneous forces generated by individuals. Its achievement seems all the more remarkable when one recalls how suppressed and constrained those forces then were by the pervasive influence of collectivist thinking on policies pursued by all parties following Britain's incomplete emergence from a war economy. The gloomy outlook for the market economy may have helped to bring together the few sharing similar views, particularly after the strength of prevailing 'Butskellism' was dramatically demonstrated by the ease with which Macmillan, as a relatively new Prime Minister, succeeded in isolating and disposing of such a strong Treasury team as Peter (later Lord) Thorneycroft, Enoch Powell and the late Nigel Birch (later Lord Rhyl). When they were allowed to resign in January 1958 on the issue of curbing government expenditure to restrain inflation, the moving spirits of the tiny IEA felt themselves alone in detecting a weakness of political will that boded ill for the future. It was about that time that Graham Hutton (a former Fabian) began to describe the Institute as 'a haven for refugees from all parties and from none'.[2]

If, from the beginning, the IEA had developed in a systematic manner, tidily implementing a detailed forward plan, it would have been out of character. There were no plans then, and there are few records now. It is already difficult to trace what happened in the years before the successful launch in 1960 of the *Hobart Paper* series—which have become the flagship of the IEA line. And though it now seems obvious that the best direction for the young IEA to travel was to concentrate on publication, *then* it was not so clear. The earliest brochure, published in 1957, mentioned schemes to help public speakers by preparing notes, to distribute articles to newspapers, and to supply lecturers to all who wished to hear them. In a manner not specified, the new Institute further hoped 'to make available the works of the great economists so that they may the more easily

[2] The early members of the Advisory Council included two other former Fabians (Dr Colin Clark and Professor Eric Nash), two with strong Liberal associations (Sir Oscar Hobson and Lord Grantchester), and George Schwartz, who was regarded as, if anything, conservative.

be brought to the notice of the public'. An early project, too, was the mock-up of a journal, dated Autumn 1957, to come out quarterly and to cost 2s. 6d. No journal appeared until 1980 and it then cost £2·45 per issue.

The Institute thus developed rather differently from the way expected, and eventually it was its own publication programme—nearly 300 titles by the middle of 1981—which was to absorb its energies and become its most effective instrument for attacking the original bold aim of 'promoting a better understanding of economic principles as they apply to the leading issues of public policy'.

A GOOD DEED

Before it could embark on its task, the IEA required a constitution, somewhere to live, staff and money.

The original Trust Deed was signed on 9 November 1955 by 'the Founders'—Antony Fisher, John Harding and Oliver Smedley—who desired

> 'to establish a charitable body to be known as the Institute of Economic Affairs . . . with the object of educating the British public in knowledge of economic and social problems and their solutions . . .'.

The IEA was governed by this Trust Deed until it became incorporated on 29 March 1963 as the IEA Limited, a private company limited by guarantee but not having a share capital, and enjoying charitable status. The three Founders gave way to seven subscribers, who all happily survive: Professor Alan Prest, Graham Hutton, Oliver Smedley, Antony Fisher, Ralph Harris, Arthur Seldon and John Wood. The only subsequent change has been to drop the word 'Limited' from the title, by a special licence dated 17 June 1974.

Curiously, the original Institute publication was not only produced, but had nearly sold out, before the IEA enjoyed a legal existence. It was in June 1955, five months before the Trust Deed was signed, that *The Free Convertibility of Sterling* by George Winder was published, with a short introduction signed by the then Director of the Institute of Economic Affairs—Antony Fisher. Thanks in part to a notable review in *Newsweek* by Henry Hazlitt, 2,000 copies were soon sold. This pioneering Paper was one of the first calls for the abolition of exchange control which had then already been prolonged for 10 years after the end of the war, and had become built into the machinery of economic planning. The call was repeated 25 years later in an IEA Research Monograph (No. 33) called *Exchange Control for Ever?*, and *post hoc, propter hoc* or not, abolition took place eight months' later!

Although other authors were approached, no further publication took place for two years, and it seemed as if, after a brisk start, the Institute had stalled on take-off. Nevertheless, if one traces the origins of the IEA back to the signing of its Trust Deed, the 25th birthday formally took place in November 1980.

But 1956 was a blank year, and there was little outward sign of continuous activity until well into 1957. The problem, of course, was to find not just someone, but exactly the right someone, to run the Institute full-time. Antony Fisher was a businessman, not an academic, and only if his business prospered could he help the IEA financially. Remembering their original meeting, and encouraged by the early success of his pioneering Buxted Chicken, Antony Fisher offered the post of

Director to Ralph Harris, and the Trustees confirmed this decision at their second meeting in July 1956. At that moment it was not possible, however, for Ralph Harris quickly to dis-entangle himself from Scotland, where he was working on the *Glasgow Herald*, after seven years' lecturing at St Andrews University. Not until January 1957 had the Institute a General Director (at £600 per annum—the rest of an income to be earned from freelance journalism), backed by £1,000 in the bank, jointly donated by Antony Fisher and Sir Robert (later Lord) Renwick. Measured by this event, the Institute's silver jubilee will take place in January 1982.

SOME GOOD ADDRESSES

Until the end of 1958, the IEA lived with its Custodian Trustee, Oliver Smedley's Investment and General Management Services, at 24 Austin Friars, a few yards from The Stock Exchange. Space was exceptionally scarce in the City at that time, and the General Director, on taking post in January 1957, found himself occupying a room so small that it could not comfortably accommodate a visitor, let alone more staff. All the same, four titles were issued from Austin Friars while attempts were being made to find somewhere else to live. In December 1958, the IEA left the City, which is to say that the General Director and sole employee took a taxi and a few files to Hobart Place in Belgravia.

The IEA worked underground in the damp basement of 7 Hobart Place for just over two years before coming up for air in February 1961 to the top floor of Eaton House, at the other end of Eaton Square, where for eight years it enjoyed a magnificent view over the trees of the square, looking towards the office it had just left.

The move to Lord North Street, the home of the IEA since May 1969, seems to be yet another gesture by the invisible hand, since its location and size so exactly suit the purposes of the Institute—and the property became available entirely by chance at exactly the right moment. (But the late Professor Harry Johnson was worried that, by moving to Westminster, the IEA might be too close to politics. And it was the same apprehension that prevented the introduction of *Westminster* Papers to follow *Hobart* and *Eaton*.)

But it was working underground, in both senses, at Hobart Place that 'made' the Institute. Before leaving for Eaton House, nine *Hobart Papers* had been published, which firmly established the series, now approaching its 90th title, of which the cover continues to show the eponymous terrace as it existed while the IEA was there. The buildings were demolished in the mid-1960s.

SOME GOOD PEOPLE

At Hobart Place the nucleus of the present team was recruited. One of Joan Culverwell's early tasks on arriving in January 1959 as Ralph Harris's secretary was to buy the first furniture and typewriter the IEA ever owned. Michael Solly arrived on a temporary assignment in May 1959, to assist with the research project that led to *A Survey of Large Companies*, and is still at work on quite a different job—that of controlling the production of all Institute material. Later recruits included John Blundell in 1962, George Polanyi in 1966, and Ken Smith, who has been IEA Librarian since 1969.

Arthur Seldon, having acted informally as editorial

adviser almost from the earliest publication which he wrote in early 1957, joined as part-time Editorial Director in June 1959, and became full-time in July 1961. By that time he and Ralph Harris had spent three years preparing the way ahead. Although only four publications were produced by the end of 1958, the rapid success of IEA titles from 1959 testified to the thoroughness of these preparations.

In the early days it was impossible to distinguish the separate contributions of Harris and Seldon to a joint effort which included the shared authorship of 10 publications in 20 years. But as Arthur Seldon took increasing charge of the publication programme, Ralph Harris was freed to address student audiences and to forge stronger links with subscribers, reviewers and other potential allies, deploying those talents as an intellectual entrepreneur in the IEA, and beyond—as, for instance, in the independent University College at Buckingham—which were recognised—to his own astonishment—in 1979 by a life peerage. At a dinner to mark the Institute's 20th birthday in January 1977, Ralph Harris told the audience of economists, journalists, businessmen and politicians not 'to mistake the front man for the show'. Drawing a comparison with Harris and Sheldon the shopfitters, he said: 'If I'm dressing the window it is Arthur [Seldon] who is stuffing good things on the shelves'.

To keep the shelves full required not only a growing effort to recruit new authors to commission, but also finding someone who could work on subjects important to the IEA for which no author could be found. George Polanyi, who joined at the end of 1966 and stayed until he died in 1975, met this challenge in a manner which was invaluable to the IEA. His versatility, and the speed with which he could—working always with his wife, Priscilla—produce a first-class brief on any subject, is reflected in the nine IEA studies published under his name—and the one which is not. His first Paper, criticising the National Plan,[3] was published under the only *nom-de-plume* the IEA has ever allowed—'Spartacus'—because he was still a captive employee of the North Western Gas Board, awaiting liberation by the IEA. The best tribute that can be paid is that it has proved impossible to replace him.

Special mention ought also to be made of John (G.E.) Blundell, who joined in September 1962, largely at his own insistence. At that time the IEA had barely published 30 titles, and was still struggling to establish itself. But John Blundell found himself so enthused by its objectives that he cut short his retirement and converted a part-time unpaid job into a full-time unpaid job until not long before his death in 1972. Formally Company Secretary, most of his time was devoted to helping to tackle what was—and remains—the indispensable requirement, raising enough money to finance well-produced publications that could be sold at prices students and teachers could afford.

In the beginning, it was particularly uphill work. Adam Smith, musing on the old proverb 'money makes money', correctly observed:

> 'When you have got a little, it is often easy to get more. The great difficulty is to get that little.'[4]

[3] *Growth through Competition: an Alternative to the National Plan,* Hobart Paper 35, 1966 (2nd Edn., 1969).

[4] *The Wealth of Nations*, Book One, Chapter IX.

The 'little' which was collected from subscriptions, donations and fees in the year to April 1958, was just £3,000. By the time John Blundell had left, the annual income was over £100,000, to which expansion his contacts and efforts had contributed greatly.

An early attempt to introduce an annual subscription for the IEA's publications—at two guineas—was set aside while the Institute flirted unsuccessfully with half-a-dozen publishers, trying to entice them into taking on the chores of marketing and distribution. But it soon became clear that the market was so specialised and, at that stage, so small, that enthusiastic marketing would be undertaken only by the IEA, and a general subscription scheme was introduced early in 1960, at five guineas annually, rising to 10 guineas in 1973, and £15 in 1979.

From its earliest days, the IEA prided itself on implementing its market principles by selling its publications and so securing a higher proportion of its income from sales than such rival groups as NIESR and PEP (as it was then called). But it was not until 1967 that the number of individual subscribers exceeded the modest total of 500. The bulk of financial support therefore had to come (as it does to this day) from commercial and industrial companies and charitable trusts, through annual donations and covenants worth about £300,000.[5] From the start, incidentally, the Institute made a virtue of not seeking or accepting taxpayers' money through grant or subsidy—a rare achievement amongst all British research organisations,

[5] The list of supporters is reproduced in the Institute's *Progress Report*.

whether engaged in the study of economic or other affairs.

SOME GOOD BOOKS

The greater the success in building up income and finding suitable staff and offices, the more scope the IEA enjoyed to develop its publications programme. Although the programme has come to be identified particularly with the *Hobart Papers*, more than four years elapsed between the original Trust Deed and the appearance of the first *Hobart Paper* in February 1960.

The hiatus is explained partly by inactivity in 1956, and the need for preparatory work in 1957. The problem was not so much shortage of money for publications, but lack of authors spontaneously moved to offer to join in the challenges to prevailing complacency about the statist drift of economic policy. Thanks to Lord Grantchester's Liberal links, Arthur Seldon was introduced to Ralph Harris, who discussed with him the re-invigorated IEA's first Paper, *Pensions in a Free Society*, published with Adam Smith's head on the cover in July 1957. The jacket blurb promised: 'Here the reader will find arguments that will not be voiced by the advocates of rival political "insurance" schemes'. Thus the early IEA publications set the pattern of rigorous and independent analysis, clarity of exposition and forthright conclusions for public policy, which have become the hallmark of all subsequent Papers under Arthur Seldon's firm editorial direction.

That first publication also brought Harris and Seldon together in fruitful partnership as joint authors. On issues in public debate where the market economist's view was swamped by conventional party and sectional pleading, Harris and Seldon would look around for authoritative economist-writers, and when the search proved vain in the early years, they joined as co-authors, for example, of *Hire Purchase in a Free Society* (1958) and *Advertising in a Free Society* (1959). It was the immediate success of these early textbooks that attracted the attention of businessmen—who could help with finance—and of academic economists who shared the authors' unorthodox approach and were encouraged to come into the open as authors of what became a rapidly growing stream of rigorous IEA critiques of the ruling consensus.

SOME GOOD TITLES

Throughout 1958 and 1959, the IEA also began by feeling its way with other kinds of publications. Originally, there was no plan for a pattern of publications consisting of several series of Papers. Rather, the idea was to issue *ad hoc* books and reports, different in size and format, though identifiable by the imprint of Adam Smith on the cover—and the first nine titles were of this kind. Before the first Hobart in February 1960, the IEA had already begun to be identified with 'those Free Society books', *viz. Pensions in a . . ., Hire Purchase in a . . ., Trade Unions in a . . .* and (a particular success) *Advertising in a . . . .* It was only in October 1959 that the idea emerged from Arthur Seldon's fertile imagination to launch a *series* of Papers, later christened *'Hobart Papers'* by Ralph Harris. By the end of 1959, 10 authors had already been commissioned to write what a reviewer of the first *Hobart Paper* described as 'academic polemics' against emotional attitudes on neglected aspects of economic policy.

Until 1966 or so, several further hard cover books were produced alongside the various series of 'Papers', published as Hobarts (from 1960), Occasionals and Eatons (from 1963), and Research Monographs (from 1966). Eventually, however, hard cover books were only published in association with a commercial publisher: the Institute concentrated on publishing and distributing its own series of Papers. By 1966, the list of titles included 28 books and 66 'Papers'; 10 years later there were only a few more books, but over 110 more Papers, including a new series of Readings (from 1967).

With the publication programme under way, an organisation nourished by a small but gently rising income, the IEA appears, in retrospect, to have been going well by the end of 1960. At the time, however, it seemed and felt differently. There was not only a financial 'crisis' in 1962, but for years the climate of opinion was entirely hostile. The IEA's work was either ignored or dismissed as 'irrelevant' by self-confident, fine-tuning, neo-Keynesian, macro-minded 'growthmen' and other collectivists, who dominated both the media and academia.

Perhaps the IEA eventually succeeded *because* opinion was then so unbalanced. In public affairs, a one-way pendulum cannot maintain itself indefinitely, and it in no way detracts from the achievement to say that in 1955-60 Britain was ready for an IEA. An economic opportunity existed, waiting to be exploited by anyone who dared to put the neglected alternative points of view to the prevailing consensus. However obvious the opportunity seems now, only the IEA went for it then, guided by the vision, foresight—and doggedness—of Ralph Harris and Arthur Seldon, always encouraged by Antony Fisher. If that appears to claim too much, one may ask in which other organisation was the case being made out for the market alternative before, say, 1964? Who else, in those years, dared to doubt the value of a National Plan or was prepared to defend the rôle of advertising, hire-purchase, the City, or industrial entrepreneurs? It was the heyday of 'price-less' economics, expressed in the language of national income specialists, for whom the debate was confined to the manipulation of large aggregates, apparently unresponsive to changes in cost or price. To argue for the use of the market (or for the price mechanism, as it was then more usually called), was to put yourself outside serious discussion into an archaic and isolated no-man's land where, incidentally, few British academics were to be found, even as explorers. But there were a few, and the IEA soon met them.[6]

To perceive the need to restore the balance of the discussion is one thing, to persevere against the odds for years is more difficult. From the beginning, however, those associated with the IEA have always been clear about the decisive influence of intellectuals and their ideas—not least Antony Fisher, who is fond of the phrase 'ideas have consequences', and part of whose contribution has been to urge the need to back that insight with documentation, academic analysis and

[6] The list would include, amonst others, Lionel Robbins, John Jewkes, Victor Morgan, Graham Hutton, and many of the early IEA authors, as well as journalists like Oscar Hobson, Paul Bareau and Harold Wincott.

independent, non-party argument. It is not surprising that the IEA's favourite paragraph in Keynes's *General Theory* makes precisely the same point:

> 'The ideas of economists and political philosophers, both when they are right and when they are wrong, are more powerful than is commonly understood. Indeed the world is ruled by little else. Practical men, who believe themselves to be quite exempt from any intellectual influences, are usually the slaves of some defunct economist.'

The quotation has been copied out, framed, and hangs on the wall of the waiting room at 2, Lord North Street.

What could not have been foreseen was the extent of the unsatisfied demand for the sort of ideas the IEA began to market. Time and again a Paper putting a totally neglected, or largely unexpressed, point of view provoked letters along the line of '. . . I thought I must have been the only person left who thought in this way . . .' or '. . . I had come to the conclusion that I was simply out of touch and unable to understand modern thinking . . .' Evidently, intellectual isolation had been the fate of many in the universities, schools, newspapers and business, who soon began to rally round the standard once the IEA had raised it. Mr Enoch Powell used to say how encouraged he had been to recognise his 'old friend the two times table'. The movement grew in strength as supporters began to realise they were not as isolated as they had imagined.

The desperate search for authors became easier after 1960 as Arthur Seldon found economists shyly volunteering to write for the IEA. And after the initial difficulties in trying to recruit a minimum of three Trustees, the Institute was eventually able to attract such outstanding scholars as Graham Hutton, Sir Sydney

Caine, John Jewkes, George Allen and Stanley Dennison, as past or present Trustees, as well as prominent businessmen.

SOME (MORE) GOOD FORTUNE

The feeling of intellectual isolation never seriously threatened the pioneers of the IEA, but only perhaps because good fortune again played its part. During 1948, Antony Fisher had written and published through Runnymede Press a short pamphlet called *The Case for Freedom*. By chance, it attracted the attention of Leonard Read and Henry Hazlitt in America, and led indirectly to an invitation to join a remarkable international group known as 'The Mont Pelerin Society' at its conference in Venice in 1954 which, in turn, led to the involvement of the IEA in the organisation of the Society's first meeting in Britain, in Oxford in 1959.

One of Joan Culverwell's first assignments on arriving at Hobart Place was to help Ralph Harris (later—1967—to become the Society's international Secretary) to arrange the Oxford meeting. Her recollection is that more of her time had to be devoted to The Mont Pelerin Society than to the Institute in the first half of 1959!

It was time well spent. The meeting brought the IEA into touch with a small group of outstanding scholars from many countries who had been brought together in 1947 by Professor Hayek

> 'to facilitate an exchange of ideas between like-minded scholars in the hope of strengthening the principles and practice of a free society and to study the working, virtues and defects of market-oriented economic systems.'

The IEA Directors were clearly at home in such a gathering, and the link with the Society, particularly with two of its Presidents—Friedrich Hayek and Milton Friedman—has been an immense source of strength. Indeed, the IEA's list of authors includes five Presidents—John Jewkes, Arthur Shenfield and George Stigler, in addition to Hayek and Friedman—and over 40 other members of the Society.

Many of them, and other 'dissident' IEA authors, may well have been surprised by the speed of change in public attitudes to what they wrote. But public opinion, like the earth, *does* move. The process is plain. What was once unthinkable can, through publication and insistent re-consideration, be made thinkable. It remains politically impossible only until time makes it politically advantageous, then urgently necessary, ending up, once the failure of policies based on the old consensus can no longer be concealed, as, at worst, a long overdue reform. In Hayek's words:

> '. . . once the more active part of the intellectuals have been converted to a set of beliefs, the process by which these become generally accepted is almost automatic and irresistible'.[7]

Yesterday's dissent becomes today's consensus.

* * *

My own connection with the IEA has enabled me to watch what happened at close quarters, and chance and coincidence again played a large part in shaping that

[7] From 'The Intellectuals and Socialism', reprinted in *Studies in Philosophy, Politics and Economics,* Routledge & Kegan Paul, 1967, p. 182.

connection. Well over 30 years ago, Ralph Harris and I met at Cambridge and went to the same tutor for economics, Stanley Dennison, for many years now a Trustee of the Institute. On coming down, we found ourselves, quite by chance, working within a few hundred yards of each other for different parts of the Conservative Party organisation—Ralph Harris as one of R. A. Butler's education officers, myself for the Research Department, where one visitor in about 1948 was Antony Fisher—already and rightly concerned about the shortcomings of Tory thinking on economic policy at the time.

Ten years later, on Ralph Harris's return from Scotland in January 1957, the IEA's first office in Austin Friars happened to be a mere hundred yards from the merchant bank in which I was then working and, again by coincidence, we both moved to Belgravia within a few weeks of each other: Ralph Harris to Hobart Place, myself to Associated Electrical Industries in Grosvenor Place, only 200 yards away. No doubt my proximity made me a useful choice (for signing cheques!) as an early Trustee of the Institute—which ended when I left the 'gentlemen' to join the 'players' and started to work (at first part-time) for the Institute in 1969. But the IEA was by then well on its way, and not even my arrival could stop it!

CHRONOLOGY OF THE IEA

1945	Antony Fisher read a summary of F. A. Hayek's *Road to Serfdom.*
1946	Fisher talked to Hayek at the LSE.*
1949	Fisher met Ralph Harris at East Grinstead.
1955 *June*	Publication of *The Free Convertibility of Sterling* by George Winder.
1955 *November*	Original Trust Deed signed by Fisher, John Harding and Oliver Smedley.
1956 *June*	Harris came from Scotland to discuss with Fisher the direction of the Institute.
1956 *July*	Trustees confirmed appointment of Harris as General Director.
1956 *October*	Lord Grantchester approached Arthur Seldon about writing a Paper on pensions for the Institute.
1957 *January*	Harris began work as (part-time) General Director at Austin Friars.

*The intellectual influence of Hayek (and Robbins) dates from 1934 at the LSE where Arthur Seldon was an undergraduate.

1957	*February*	Harris and Seldon met at 4 Dean's Yard, Westminster.
1957	*July*	Publication of *Pensions in a Free Society*.
1958		Seldon appointed Editorial Adviser.
1958	*January*	Publication of *Hire Purchase in a Free Society*. Second edition in July 1959 edited by Harris, Seldon and Margot Naylor. Third, rewritten, in February 1961.
1958	*September*	Publication of *The City's Invisible Earnings* by W. M. Clarke.
1958	*December*	Publication of *The Future of the Sterling System* by Paul Bareau.
1958	*December*	Institute moved to basement in Hobart Place with offices for Harris, Seldon, Joan Culverwell (from January 1959) and Michael Solly (from May 1959).
1959	*February*	Publication of *Advertising in a Free Society*.
1959	*June*	Seldon appointed part-time Editorial Director.
1959	*June*	Publication of *Trade Unions in a Free Society* by B. C. Roberts.
1959	*September*	Fisher, Harris and Joan Culverwell helped to organise the Oxford Conference of the Mont Pelerin Society.
1959	*October*	*Survey of Large Companies*, by Harris and Solly, published.

1959 *December*	Seldon proposed a series of Papers for economists to explore the market approach to issues of the day: eventually emerged as the *Hobart Papers*; nearly 90 had been published by Spring 1981.
1960 *January*	Publication of *Not Unanimous—A Rival Verdict to Radcliffe's on Money.*
1960 *February*	Publication of first *Hobart Paper.*
1960 *May*	Publication of *Trade with Communist Countries* by Alec Nove and Desmond Donnelly.
1960 *June*	Publication of *Saving in a Free Society* by Enoch Powell.
1961 *February*	IEA moved to Eaton Square.
1961 *July*	Seldon appointed full-time Editorial Director.
1962 *April*	A financial crisis. Harris and Seldon downed tools (pens) and concentrated on fund-raising for three months.
1962	Harris proposed the *Eaton Papers* to analyse the economics of information. Nine were published between 1963 and 1966.
1962	Seldon proposed a field study into public preferences between state and private welfare services. Four reports on *Choice in Welfare*, 1963, 1965, 1970 and 1978, assembled in *Over-Ruled on Welfare*, 1979.

1962	*September*	John Blundell joined part-time.
1963	*March*	IEA incorporated as the Institute of Economic Affairs Limited, a private company limited by guarantee.
1963	*April*	John Wood appointed Trustee.
1963	*November*	The first *Occasional Paper* (by George Stigler). 59 published by early 1981.
1965	*May*	The first of 12 *Key Discussion Books* intended for Sixth Form teaching.
1966	*January*	George Polanyi joined as non-resident, full-time researcher.
1966	*January*	Dinner to celebrate IEA's 10th year, attended by 150 academics, businessmen and writers: principal addresses by Professor John Jewkes, Sir Paul Chambers and Lord Robbins reproduced in Occasional Paper 8, *Economics, Business and Government*.
1966	*January*	Solly proposed a series of *Research Monographs*. 35 published by early 1981.
1967		Harris became Hon. Sec. of the Mont Pelerin Society and organised the meeting at Aviemore in 1968 and the Adam Smith Double Centenary Meeting at St. Andrews University in 1976.
1967	*June*	The first *IEA Readings*. 25 published by the end of 1980.

1967-68	'Hobart lunches' gradually evolved into discussions addressed by a visiting economist and presided over by Harris.
1968 *February*	The first of 4 *Background Memoranda* was published.
1968 *December*	Harris and Seldon drafted *The Urgency of an Independent University*, signed by 45 British scholars. (A 2nd Edn., in November 1969, listed 100 signatories.)
1969	Wood joined staff part-time.
1969 *April*	Harris initiated the Wincott Foundation in memory of Harold Wincott, to sponsor annual lectures and prizes for economic journalists. By 1981 11 Wincott Lectures had been published as *Occasional Papers*.
1969 *May*	IEA moved to Lord North Street.
1970	Seldon proposed the *Hobart Paperbacks* to analyse the transition from ideas to policy. 13 published by the end of 1980.
1971 *July*	Wood appointed full-time Deputy Director.
1972 *June*	The first of (so far) 11 one-day seminars, for IEA subscribers in industry, government, schools and universities, etc. The proceedings were published in *IEA Readings*.

1972	Wood established the first of several agencies for overseas distribution of IEA Papers.
1976 *January*	Harris appointed Hon. Sec. of the Political Economy Club.
1976 *February*	University College at Buckingham opened to students.
1977 *January*	*Not from benevolence . . .*, written by Harris and Seldon in six weeks (and prepared and produced by Solly and printers in 14 working days), published to mark IEA's 20th anniversary.
1979 *June*	Harris raised to the peerage.
1980 *July*	Harris proposed creation of the Patrick Hutber Memorial, a residence for students at the University College, Buckingham.
1980 *September*	Seldon appointed to Board of the Mont Pelerin Society.
1980 *October*	The first number of *The Journal of Economic Affairs* (quarterly) was published by Basil Blackwell, edited by Seldon.
1980 *December*	Social Affairs Unit formed: Director, Digby C. Anderson; Assistant Director, David Marsland.

LIST OF IEA AUTHORS, 1957-81

Acton, H. B.
Addison, J. T.
Alchian, Armen A.
Alexander, Andrew
Allen, G. C.
Allen, William R.
Altman, Wilfred
Anderson, Digby

Bacon, Robert
Bareau, Paul
Barran, D. H.
Bauer, P. T.
Bays, Anthony
Beales, A. C. F.
Bealey, Frank
Beckerman, Wilfred
Beenstock, Michael
Beesley, M. E.
Benham, Frederic
Blaug, Mark
Bowley, Marian
Boyson, Rhodes
Bracewell-Milnes, J. B.
Brealey, R. A.
Bremner, Marjorie
Brennan, H. Geoffrey
Breton, Albert
Brittan, Samuel
Brown, E. H. Phelps
Brunner, John
Buchanan, J. M.
Budd, Alan
Burn, Duncan
Burney, Sir Anthony
Burton, John

Caine, Sir Sydney
Cairncross, Sir Alec
Canes, Michael
Cannon, Peter
Carmichael, John
Carter, R. L.
Cave, Merrie
Chaloner, W. H.
Chambers, Sir Paul
Cheung, Steven N. S.
Chiplin, Brian
Chown, John
Christopher, Anthony

Clark, Colin
Clarke, W. M.
Coats, A. W.
Collard, David
Colquhoun, Iain
Congdon, Tim
Cooper, M. H.
Coyne, John
Crew, Michael A.
Cromer, Lord
Csikós-Nagy, Béla
Culyer, A. J.
Curtin, Timothy
Cyriax, George

Davies, Alun G.
Davies, Christie
Deaglio, Mario
de Jouvenel, Bertrand
Denman, D. R.
Denman, S. E.
Donges, Jeurgen B.
Donnelly, Desmond
Drake, K. B.
Duncan, Sir Val
Dunning, John H.
du Sautoy, Peter

Eden, Douglas
Edey, Harold
Edinburgh, The Duke of
Elkan, Walter
Elst, Philip Vander,
Eltis, Walter
Evans, Sir Lincoln

Farrell, M. J.
Feather, Lord (Victor)
Ferns, H. S.
Fisher, Malcolm
Flemming, John
Fletcher, Raymond
Fogarty, Michael P.
Foster, Christopher
Frankel, S. Herbert
Fraser, Ian
Frey, Bruno
Friedman, Milton
Fulop, Christina

Gash, Norman
Gélinier, Octave
Gibson, N. J.
Gough, T. J.
Gould, Julius
Grant, Robert
Gray, Hamish
Greenaway, David
Griffiths, Brian
Grimond, Jo
Grugeon, Sir John
Grunfeld, Cyril

Haberler, G.
Hallett, Graham
Hannah, Leslie

Hanson, C. G.
Harbury, Colin D.
Harris, Anthony
Harris, Ralph
Hartley, Keith
Hartwell, R. M.
Hayek, F. A.
Heath, J. B.
Henderson, P. D.
Henderson, R. F.
Henderson, W. O.
Hennessy, Jossleyn
Herbert, A. P.
Hibbs, John
Hicks, Sir John
Hicks, Lady Ursula
Hindley, Brian
Hobson, Sir Oscar
Hoos, Ida R.
Houghton, Lord (Douglas)
Howarth, Richard W.
Howe, Sir Geoffrey
Howell, David
Hutchison, T. W.
Hutt, W. H.
Hutton, Graham

Ilersic, A. R.
Ingram, Stuart
Ireland, Marilyn J.
Ireland, Thomas R.

Jackman, Richard
Jacoby, Neil H.
James, G. R.
James, Gwyn
Jay, Douglas
Jay, Peter
Jefferson, Michael
Jervis, F. R.
Jewkes, John
Johnson, David B.
Johnson, Harry G.
Johnson, Nevil
Johnson, P. S.
Jones, George W.
Joseph, Sir Keith
Judge, Ken

Kahn, Lord (Richard)
Keegan, William
Kellett, Richard
Kelly, Terence
Kemp, Arthur
King, D. N.
King, Wilfred
Kirzner, Israel
Klappholz, Kurt
Knight, Sir Arthur
Knox, Frank
Koch, James V.
Kogan, Maurice

Lachmann, L. M.
Laidler, David
Lait, June
Lawson, Nigel

Layton, David
Lees, D. S.
Leijonhufvud, Axel
Lepage, Henri
Lewis, Alan
Lewis, W. R.
Lichfield, Nathaniel
Lincoln, John A.
Ling, A. G.
Littlechild, S. C.
Lutz, Vera
Lynn, Richard

McCord, Norman
McKendrick, Neil
McKie, Robert
MacRae, D. G.
McRae, Hamish
Macrae, Norman
Manser, W. A. P.
Marlow, Barbara
Marquand, David
Marsland, David
Masefield, Sir Peter
Mathias, Peter
Maynard, A. K.
Meade, J. E.
Miller, Harry
Miller, Margaret
Miller, Robert
Milner, Christopher
Minford, A. P. L.
Mingay, G. E.
Mishan, E. J.
Moohr, Michael
Morgan, Ann D.
Morgan, David R.
Morgan, E. Victor
Murray, David
Myddelton, David R.
Myers, Robert J.

Nash, E. F.
Nash, John E.
Naylor, Guy
Naylor, Margot
Neal, Sir Leonard
Nishiyama, Chiaki
Niskanen, William A.
Noble, Pat
Norton, Graham
Nove, Alec

Okabe, Mitsuaki
Okano, Yukihide
Oppenheimer, P. M.
O'Brien, Denis P.

Paish, F. W.
Papps, Ivy
Pardoe, John
Parkin, Michael
Parkinson, Stephen
Peacock, Alan T.
Pearce, Ivor
Pennance, F. G.

Pepper, Gordon T.
Perlman, Morris
Perry, George
Peston, Maurice H.
Peters, G. H.
Piotrowicz, Teresa M.
Plant, Sir Arnold
Polanyi, George
Ponsonby, G. J.
Powell, J. Enoch
Prentice, Reg
Prest, A. R.
Psacharopoulos, George

Ramsey, James B.
Randall, Peter
Ratcliff, A. R. N.
Reekie, W. Duncan
Rees, Albert
Rees-Mogg, William
Reynolds, D. J.
Ricketts, Martin,
Ridley, Nicholas
Rimmer, Douglas
Robbins, Lord (Lionel)
Roberts, Ben
Robertson, D. J.
Robinson, Sir Austin
Robinson, Colin
Robinson, T. K.
Roche, J. W.
Rose, Harold
Roth, G. J.
Rouse, James
Rowley, Charles K.
Rydenfelt, Sven

Salsbury, A. J.
Sandford, C. T.
Savage, George
Sawers, David
Scarman, Lord
Schaffer, R.
Scimone, G.
Seale, J. R.
Seldon, Arthur
Senior, Ian
Sewill, Brendon
Sharrock, W. W.
Shawcross, Lord
Shenfield, A. A.
Shenfield, Barbara
Shenoy, Sudha
Sirc, Ljubo
Slesser, Sir Henry
Sloane, P. J.
Slough, D. G.
Smith, Henry
Solly, Michael
Stigler, George J.
Streissler, E. W.

Tanzi, Vito
Taylor, T. W.
Telser, Lester G.
Thomas, Denis

Thomson, Norman
Thorneycroft, Peter
Treasure, J. A. P.
Tugendhat, Georg
Tullock, Gordon

Usher, Dan

Vaubel, Roland
Veale, Sir Douglas
Vice, Anthony
Vinson, Nigel

Wagner, R. E.
Walters, A. A.
Ward, Barbara
Watkins, J. W. N.
Watrin, Christian
Wells, Sidney, J.
West, E. G.
West, W. A.
Whetstone, Linda
Whiteley, Paul
Whyte, Lewis
Wickenden, Keith
Williams, J. E. Ffowcs
Wilson, Charles
Wilson, Tom
Wincott, Harold
Wiseman, Jack
Wood, Geoffrey E.
Wood, John B.

Yamey, B. S.
Yarrow, George
Young, Alistair

INDEX OF MAIN THEMES
and related concepts and subjects

INDEX TO AUTHORS CITED
and other sources and references
(IEA authors listed pp. 271-6)